DATE			

Kipling
Interviews and Recollections

Volume 1

Also by Harold Orel

THE WORLD OF VICTORIAN HUMOR
SIX ESSAYS IN NINETEENTH-CENTURY ENGLISH
LITERATURE AND THOUGHT *(with George J. Worth)*
THOMAS HARDY'S EPIC-DRAMA: A Study of *The Dynasts*
THOMAS HARDY'S PERSONAL WRITINGS *(editor)*
THE DEVELOPMENT OF WILLIAM BUTLER YEATS:
1885–1900
BRITISH POETRY 1880–1920: Edwardian Voices *(with Paul Wiley)*
THE NINETEENTH-CENTURY WRITER AND HIS
AUDIENCE *(with George J. Worth)*
ENGLISH ROMANTIC POETS AND THE ENLIGHTEN-
MENT
IRISH HISTORY AND CULTURE: Aspects of a People's
Heritage
THE FINAL YEARS OF THOMAS HARDY, 1912–1928
THOMAS HARDY: *The Dynasts*, New Wessex Edition *(editor)*
THE SCOTTISH WORLD *(with Marilyn Stokstad and Henry L. Snyder)*

KIPLING

Interviews and Recollections

Volume 1

Edited by

Harold Orel

Barnes & Noble Books
Totowa, New Jersey

Selection and editorial matter © Harold Orel 1983
1983

First published in the U.S.A. 1983 by
BARNES & NOBLE BOOKS
81, Adams Drive, Totowa
New Jersey, 07512

ISBN 0-389-20275-4

Printed in Hong Kong

Library of Congress Cataloging in Publication Data

Main entry under title:

Kipling, interviews and recollections.

1. Kipling, Rudyard, 1865–1936—Interviews. 2. Authors,
English—19th century—Interviews. 3. Authors, English—20th
century—Interviews. I. Orel, Harold, 1926–
PR4856.K49   828'.809   82–1724
ISBN 0-389-20275-4   AACR2

To Alan and Mary Bassett

Contents

PART IV   SUCCESS IN ENGLAND

Preface

Kipling's personality had a powerful impact on all kinds of people, and he met more of them, and in more widely-scattered corners of the world, than most writers. His natural instinct for speaking out on controversial issues made it difficult for those who did not know him at first-hand to make allowances for his diffidence (which was genuine), or for his willingness to compromise when out-argued or persuasively shown the error of his logic. Many readers became enthusiastic, angry, disgusted; it was difficult to remain neutral about Kipling the man when Kipling's writings attacked an exposed nerve.

Yet to this day it is difficult to see Kipling plain. As a journalist in India, and in the various countries to which he had been sent on assignment, he appreciated the need for getting at the facts even if those in positions of authority found it expedient to deny him access. He believed that character was the key to much public policy, and he delighted in the personalities of writers. But he treasured privacy and insulted reporters who infringed on what he considered to be private matters; moved from one home to another because curiosity about his affairs became too insistent; and finally retreated to Bateman's, his seventeenth-century home in the village of Burwash, Sussex. Bateman's was not easy to reach; but then Kipling did not want it to be.

Those who call Kipling an 'imperialist' and 'jingo' as if the two terms are loosely interchangeable do not pay much attention to the changing phases of his career. Some critics succumb easily to the temptation to use the life to explicate the art, and the art to illuminate the life. There exists a very deep chasm between the disdain or disapproval of a very large number of literary critics, historians, and representatives of the Establishment, and the worldwide popularity of Kipling's works. Kipling's life and career remain puzzling despite the passage of almost half a century since his burial in Westminster Abbey.

The following selections, which have been culled from a vast literature of Kiplingiana, will provide an interested public with assessments made by a large number of individuals who knew Kipling. Cast in the form of interviews and recollections, these essays, which range in length from a few paragraphs to fairly substantial statements, provide a great deal of information about Kipling's family background, his formative years in India and at Westward Ho!, his journalistic assignments, his sensational début in London society in the early 1890s, his curiously ambivalent relationship with the United States, his restless (almost feverish) travels, his growing international fame, his involvement with political and social issues, his family tragedies and his health problems, and his life during the eighteen years that followed the Great War. The materials for a synthesised portrait of one of the most original, talented and remarkable writers in the history of English literature are here in God's plenty, enabling readers to see the relationship between the locales he knew and the imaginative literature he created, and to evaluate him as a man.

Here, then, is Mr Rudyard Kipling, as remembered by more than eighty men and women.

Acknowledgements

Thanks are due to the American Philosophical Society for a grant-in-aid from the Primrose Fund; to Robert P. Cobb, Executive Vice-Chancellor of the University of Kansas, and to Gerhard Zuther, Chairman of the English Department, for encouragement on this project; to Frances D. Horowitz, Vice-Chancellor for Research, Graduate Studies and Public Service, and Dean of the Graduate School, and Robert C. Bearse, Associate Vice-Chancellor in the same office, for their support, provided through the General Research Fund; to Sankaran Ravindran for his help on some problems relating to Kipling's years in India; to Mary Davidson for assistance in solving a variety of annotation questions; and to the following individuals for responding helpfully to specific inquiries: Mrs T. P. Srinivasan, William Fletcher, George Jerkovich, Oliver C. Phillips, George J. Worth, L. E. James Helyar, Eleanor Symons and Helmut Huelsbergen. Nancy Kreighbaum, Peggy Wessel and Paula Oliver prepared the manuscript.

I am grateful to those who staff the Reference Desk and take care of Inter-Library Loan Services at the University of Kansas Library, and to Alexandra Mason, Director, and William Mitchell, of the Spencer Research Library.

Special thanks are due to Julia Steward and Valery Brooks of Macmillan for their thoughtful and helpful editorial assistance.

Kipling's writings are dated in terms of their first publication, to enable readers to relate a particular poem, short story, or book to a period in his life. The basic authority used for these identifications is *Rudyard Kipling: A Bibliographical Catalogue*, by James McG. Stewart, ed. A. W. Yeats (Toronto: Dalhousie University Press and University of Toronto Press, 1959). Difficult words, phrases, topical allusions, place-names and literary references are annotated whenever possible, and to the fullest extent within space limitations. While reviewing Kipling's own writings, I have found particularly helpful the 5672 pages of *The Reader's Guide to Rudyard Kipling's Work*, prepared by Roger Lancelyn Green, Alec Mason, and especially R. E. Harbord between 1961 and 1972 (Canterbury: Gibbs & Sons; later, Bournemouth: Boscombe Printers). All persons interested in Kipling are indebted to the contents of the *Kipling Journal*, published by the Kipling Society continuously since March

1927. A notable bibliography of secondary materials – of writings about Rudyard Kipling – was compiled and edited by Helmut E. Gerber and Edward Lauterbach, and published in *English Fiction in Transition*, III, nos 3–5 (1960), and VIII, nos 3–4 (1965). Three biographies of Kipling, based on intensive research and travel as well as first-hand information, are collectively indispensable: Charles Carrington's *Rudyard Kipling* (London: Macmillan, 1955, revised in 1978); Angus Wilson's *The Strange Ride of Rudyard Kipling* (London: Secker & Warburg, 1977); and Lord Birkenhead's *Rudyard Kipling* (London: Weidenfeld & Nicolson, 1978). I regret that the scope of this work prevents me from drawing more often on the surprisingly ample literature dealing with Rudyard Kipling's parents and family. They were colourful in their own right, and superb achievers of almost anything they set out to do; fascinating information about their lives and accomplishments turns up in many memoirs. But that is another story.

In addition, the editor and publishers wish to thank the following who have kindly given permission for the use of copyright material:

The Atlantic Monthly Co., for the extract from 'The Young Kipling' by Edmonia Hill, published in *The Atlantic Monthly*, April 1936, copyright 1936 by The Atlantic Monthly Co., Boston, Mass.
The Earl Baldwin of Bewdley, for the extract from 'The Unfading Genius of Rudyard Kipling' by Arthur Windham Baldwin.
Boydell & Brewer Ltd, for the extract from *The Cloak That I Left* by Lilias Rider Haggard.
Curtis Brown Ltd, London, on behalf of Beverley Nichols, for the extract from *25: Being a Young Man's Candid Recollections of his Elders and Betters*.
Faber & Faber Ltd, for the extract from *Listening for the Drums* by Sir Ian Hamilton.
Hamish Hamilton Ltd, for the extracts from 'Kipling and Edgar Wallace' by Margaret Lane in *Edgar Wallace: The Biography of a Phenomenon*.
Harper & Row, Publishers, Inc., for the extracts from *Mark Twain in Eruption*, edited by Bernard De Voto, copyright 1940 by the Mark Twain Co.
Houghton Mifflin Co., for the extract from *A Golden Age of Authors* by William Webster Ellsworth.
John Murray (Publishers) Ltd, for the extracts from *Francis Younghusband, Explorer and Mystic* by George Seaver, and from *The*

Lost Historian: A Memoir of Sir Sidney Low by Desmond Chapman-Huston.

Oxford University Press, for the extract from *Three Houses* by Angela Thirkell.

The executors of the Estate of Dorothy C. Ponton, for the extracts from her articles published in the *Kipling Journal*.

Charles Scribner's Sons, for the extracts from *These Many Years: Recollections of a New Yorker* by Brander Matthews, copyright 1917 by Charles Scribner's Sons, and renewed in 1945.

The Vermont Country Store, for the extract from *Rudyard Kipling's Vermont Feud* by Frederic F. Van De Water.

Whilst every effort has been made to locate owners of copyright in some cases this has been unsuccessful. The publishers apologise for any infringement of copyright or failure to acknowledge original sources and shall be glad to include any necessary corrections in subsequent printings.

A Note on the Text

In the extracts given, spelling errors in the originals have been silently corrected; English forms have replaced American spellings; book titles are printed consistently in italics; and punctuation usage has been rendered uniform in accordance with English practice.

A Note on Kipling's Life

Joseph Rudyard Kipling was born in Bombay on 30 December 1865 as the son of John Lockwood Kipling, an artist of Yorkshire stock, and Alice Macdonald Kipling, who came from a family with strong artistic and cultural interests. He was sent home to England for his education, and to avoid the danger of falling ill in a tropical climate. The unhappy years of lonely childhood (1871–7) were followed by a more lively period at the United Services College, Westward Ho!, in north Devon, where he began a series of lifelong friendships. In 1882 he became a reporter, assistant editor and factotum for the widely-read *Civil and Military Gazette* of Lahore, and in 1887 he moved to *The Pioneer* of Allahabad. His short stories, originally printed as newspaper columns, were collected in *Plain Tales from the Hills*, *Soldiers Three* and *Wee Willie Winkie*.

Coming home to England a second time by way of a long sea and land voyage to Japan and the United States, Kipling rapidly became famous. After publication of *The Light that Failed* (1890), he travelled extensively: South Africa, New Zealand and Australia. His close friend, publisher and adviser, Wolcott Balestier, died in 1891; the next year Kipling married Caroline Starr Balestier, Wolcott's sister, and moved to Brattleboro, Vermont, to be near his wife's family. A series of popular books – *Barrack-Room Ballads*, *Many Inventions*, the two Jungle Books and *Captains Courageous* – appeared during the next few years; but a quarrel with Beatty Balestier, his wife's brother, led to a lawsuit, unpleasant publicity, and Kipling's decision to leave the United States for England (1896). In 1899 he fell seriously ill of lung-inflammation, and before he recovered, his much-loved elder daughter, Josephine, died.

Kipling's serious interest in the affairs of a great empire was expressed in 'Recessional', a prophetic warning published during the celebrations for Queen Victoria's Diamond Jubilee, and in his writings on the events and personalities of the Boer War. Meanwhile, his works multiplied: *Stalky & Co., Kim, Just So Stories,*

Traffics and Discoveries, Puck of Pook's Hill. In 1907 he became the first Englishman to win the Nobel Prize for Literature. In 1910 his mother died; in 1911, his father. The First World War brought further tragedy: Kipling's son John was killed during the Battle of Loos (1915). Kipling wrote a great deal about life in the services, as well as a history of his son's regiment, *The Irish Guards in the Great War*. A duty that he took very seriously was service as one of the Imperial War Graves Commissioners.

His last decade was troubled by various illnesses, and a number of his short stories dealt with pain; they were written in what was becoming known as 'the later style'. He undertook preparation of a final revised text of his collected works (the Sussex Edition). On 18 January 1936, he died from a violent haemorrhage at Middlesex Hospital. A service at Westminster Abbey was followed by burial in Poets' Corner. The following year his incomplete memoir, *Something of Myself*, was published. His widow died in 1939. Mrs George Bambridge (Elsie Kipling, the younger daughter) died in 1976.

Part I
Kipling's Family

Rudyard*

It has been stated that 'Rudyard' is a Hollandish word and derived from the ancient Teutonic, being made up of two Teutonic words – *hruod*, 'council' or 'counsel', and *gyerd*, 'a fence' or 'enclosure'; and hence it carries the meaning 'council-guard' or 'the enclosure of a conclave'. This second syllable may be compared with our own English words 'yard', 'guard', and 'garden' – all of them derived from the same Teutonic original. The Irish race, in strict conservatism of the primal sound, continue to pronounce 'guard' as 'gyarrd', and 'garden' as 'gyarrden' and 'guardian' as 'gyarrdyen'. What have our philologists to say of this derivation of Rudyard? In Winchfield, Hants, parish church are the tombstones of the 'Rudyerd' family, dating from Stuart times, the most notable being Sir Benjamin Rudyerd, who was a poet as well as politician. It has been stated frequently that Kipling was named 'Rudyard' after Rudyard Lake in Staffordshire. Here is a story that appeared in the *Kansas City Star* as told by one J. Bourne Pinder. 'My father was Thomas Pinder of the pottery firm of Pinder, Bourne and Co., now Doulton's, in Burslem,[1] Staffordshire. In the pottery was a young man named John Kipling, a designer of decorations. He was a very clever young man, although somewhat eccentric. He used, I remember, as a boy, to carry pet mice attached to him by fine chains. He was a very vigorous man, full of amusing stories, and could do innumerable tricks. When I was a boy he made casts of my face. He made paper quills and put them in my nostrils, greased my face and then covered it with wet plaster. It was no fun, I can tell you, but he was a good sort of chap and used to tell me stories and sing songs and make things with a jack-knife for me, so I let him do it. He was a constant visitor at our house, and both my mother and father were very fond of him. One day my mother gave a picnic to the young people of the neighbourhood at a pretty little English lake between the villages of Rudyard and Rushton,[2] not far from

* Unsigned article in *Kipling Journal*, VII (Dec 1940) 16.

Burslem. John Kipling went, of course, and there met a pretty English girl, named Macdonald, the daughter of a Methodist minister at Endon.[3] Kipling fell in love with her at once. They met very often at my mother's house, and it grew into a love affair on both sides. Then John Kipling went to the art schools in Kensington, and afterwards went out to direct the art schools in Lahore, and he took Miss Macdonald along with him to India as his wife. In the fullness of time a son was born to the Kiplings in Bombay. Their first meeting at Rudyard Lake must have been the pretty bit of sentiment of their lives, for when they named their son they took for him that of the little lake on the banks of which they first saw each other.'

In a letter dated 11 July 1900, to the *Manchester Daily Dispatch*, Rudyard Kipling wrote to say 'that so far as he knew there was no connection between his family and the place named Rudyard'. This seems to dispose of J. Bourne Pinder's interesting little story in the *Kansas City Star*.

NOTES

1. Burslem is one of the group of five Staffordshire towns noted for pottery; birthplace of Josiah Wedgwood, and home of the Wedgwood Institute. John Lockwood Kipling worked as an artist in the pottery, and became acquainted with Frederic Macdonald, and later Alice Macdonald.

2. Rudyard is a parish and hamlet in Staffordshire, 2 miles north-west of Leek. Rushton is a small village 4½ miles north-west of Leek.

3. In southern Worcestershire.

Some Reminiscences of my Brother*

ALICE MACDONALD FLEMING

After the 'Kipling Boom' I was often asked when I had first begun to realise that I had a genius for my only brother. I said I had always known it. I never remember him boasting as either boy or youth; he never talked of the masterpieces he hoped to write, as so many young people do (talking away their ideas instead of writing them), but I always knew that if he wished to accomplish anything he would do it. Many of the early reviews of his work rang the changes on 'conceit and cocksureness', for to a certain class of mind it was, of course, intolerable that a young writer should be so clever. Even reputable reviewers appeared to accept Dick in *The Light that Failed* as a self-portrait more accurate than pleasing. One critic fastened upon 'the Nilghai's'[1] phrase of 'a public who think with their boots and read with their elbows' as a 'leading clause in Rudyard Kipling's scornful creed', and preached a serious homily upon it. This was particularly pleasing, for the silly little phrase was a spark – struck out by me in the heat of talk and instantly 'taken' by Ruddy with the familiar 'O! good, bags I.' He has told the world in *Something of Myself* that our mother gave him what is perhaps the most frequently quoted line, 'What do they know of England who only England know?', but I was surprised to find that he had forgotten his debt to her for 'Oh East is East and West is West', etc., and still more to my father for a very great deal of 'On Greenhow Hill'. A kindly commentator has praised his accurate knowledge of Yorkshire dialect and Yorkshire geography, but the praise belongs to my father – not to my brother; we were never in Yorkshire before my father came home in 1878, and I think only once in his company.

---

* *Kipling Journal*, no. 44 (Dec 1937) 118–21. (Article signed 'Mrs J. Fleming'.)

Even before *Plain Tales* came out in book form I suffered a good deal from the type of person who used to say – at dances generally – 'I hear you're awfflly clever, Miss Kiplin' and that you write books.' The obvious reply, of course, was 'You're mistaking me for my brother, he suffers from both these complaints.' 'O, you're rottin' – what's your line then?' 'Me? – O, I'm the fool of the family.'

This brings me back to the time of which I originally meant to speak – January 1884, when the Bombay mail drew into the brickwork fortress that is Lahore Station, and my mother, always quicker than anyone else in both sight and speech, cried, 'Look, look, there's Ruddy – and there's Mrs Ibbetson, bless her!' Rudyard looked incredibly grown up to my fifteen-year-old eyes, with a real moustache, instead of the badly shaved upper lip ordered by the United Services College. His companion was a round-faced lady with a delightful smile, wife of the 'great and wise civilian who wrote the vilest hand ever seen', and who ultimately became Sir Denzil, and Governor of the Punjab. They were our lifelong friends. That was a wonderful home-coming, though the black spot in the poppy was that my father had been summoned to Calcutta to help to organise a big exhibition and did not return for some three weeks. But the beautiful room he had designed for me was waiting me, with its lacquered furniture patterned in graffito, its high dado of Indian cotton, and its charming painted fireplace where my initials were so twined among Persian flowers and arabesques that they seemed part of the design – I had never had a room of my own, really furnished for me, before, and it all seemed part of the magic. My father's pet ravens, Jack and Jill, the little grey squirrels on the 'creeper covered trellis', and my brother's bull terrier Buzz, carried on the enchantment. The ravens were almost too tame – they would sit on my shoulder, and it was some time before I learnt that their long pick-axe beaks were never used to investigate eyes or ears! The squirrels were bolder; they would sit on my book, or pull out little tufts of hair for nest lining. It was at Ruddy's suggestion that I hung up a tangle of woollen threads stolen from my mother's workbag. They understood and appreciated our good intentions at once, and selected the most suitable colours for camouflage. In a day or two only bright blue, red and purple threads were left.

My brother and I seldom rode together, for his prophetic eye always saw me returning with some terrible injury, even before I was settled in the saddle. Personally, he was fearless, and in spite of

his glasses, he played polo – secretly in order not to alarm my
mother. Tennis never attracted him.

I did not know till afterwards that before my parents risked
bringing me out to India so young they had made a compact that,
though I should not go into society until I was seventeen, I would
never be left alone in the evening when my elders went to ball or
dinner. I merely thought how nice it was that Ruddy was always
disengaged when both parents dined out. Though the games we
played on those occasions may not have been very funny in
themselves, I have never laughed so much, before or since. On a
Shakespeare evening, all talk except quotations from the Bard were
forbidden, and my chief difficulty was to check my brother's talent
for improvisation; I grew to mistrust such unassuming lines as

> My liege of Westmoreland, the pinnace stays
> To give you waftage to the further shore.

When challenged, he would airily refer me to 'the Richards' or 'the
Henrys', and, according to the rules of the game, no volume of
Shakespeare might be opened until next morning, so it was difficult
to check his references.

Many of our after-dinner games finally found shape in the little
volume *Echoes*,[2] which I do not think many of you will have seen, but
we had great fun in writing it. Many years afterwards, when my
brother was asked by a representative of the ever-rapacious
American public to include *Echoes* in a volume of his early works, he
found it difficult to disentangle my work from his. I told him I really
could not give up one of my prize efforts – a little poem in the style of
Rossetti which he thought was his, and he was quite cross about
that.

Another game we played until our parents stopped it, because
they said they were gradually losing their brains over it, was Yadasi,
a singularly charming game which my brother took from an old
magazine. One of the rules was that a player must never receive
anything from the hands of another without saying, at the moment
when he took it, 'By my knowledge.' It is quite simple, but it goes on
all the time, until one of the players dies – or goes mad. It got to such
a pitch that finally my father said it must cease; we could hardly
help ourselves to dishes at the table without murmuring, 'By my
knowledge.'

Another of my happy memories, when I was seventeen, is his taking me to dances. I persuaded him to throw off his schoolboy self-consciousness and learn to dance. I took a good deal of pains to teach him – I think I am right in saying that this did not form part of the curriculum at Westward Ho! His sense of rhythm was perfect, and the footwork was no trouble to him, but steering was always a difficulty.

I was as tall as he was and when he was in any difficulty I used to hastily change over and lead him. He gave me a very pretty bangle for all this. But, of course, he never encouraged vanity on my part, and I remember him once saying to me after a big dance, 'Mrs . . . says I am a much better dancer than you are', to which I replied, 'She was not one of my partners, ask Captain . . . for his opinion': and he was good enough to say, 'One up to you.' These nice days went on until about 1887, when my brother was promoted – a rather thrilling promotion – to go to Allahabad to be on the staff of *The Pioneer* there. I was married in 1889, so the best of the young days were over.

I shall never forget these young days, and though they really seem not much to talk about, they are very happy to look back upon.

NOTES

Alice, or 'Trix', lived from 1868 to 1948. After Rudyard left India, she married John Fleming (1858–1942), a soldier of the Queen's Own Borderers who had been seconded to the Survey Department. For an informative and sympathetic portrait of Trix, see Florence Macdonald's 'In Memoriam: Mrs Alice Macdonald Fleming', *Kipling Journal*, xvi (Apr 1949) 7–8.

1. One of the war correspondents and pressmen in *The Light that Failed*.

2. *Echoes, by Two Writers* was published at Lahore in 1884, and was bound with *Schoolboy Lyrics* (1881), printed at the Civil and Military Gazette Press.

My Brother, Rudyard Kipling (1)*

ALICE MACDONALD FLEMING

It is eleven years since my brother Rudyard Kipling died, and as the slow years lengthen I find I no longer dwell on the Kipling Boom in 1890 – delightful and amusing as was that diverting surprise – or on the rich and crowded years before sorrow and death came to his hearthstone. I take refuge rather in our very early days together when a sturdy little boy, not quite six and a spoilt baby of three and a half – that was *me* – were left by their parents, who were going back to India, to face a cold world alone. And it was a *very* cold world, without one familiar face. And we were left with strangers who were very unkind to us. I think child psychology is better understood now. No kind and loving parents would leave their children for years without giving them any preparation or explanation.

As it was, we felt deserted – everything had gone at once. Mama, Papa, our home in a garden full of sunshine and birds. Dear Ayah, who was never cross; clever Meeta, our bearer, who made toys out of oranges and nuts; Dunnoo, who took care of the fat white pony which Ruddy *would* call Dapple Gray; and Chokra, the boy who called the other servants and only grinned and didn't mind when I pelted him with my bricks. All gone at one swoop – and why? 'Aunty' – as we called the woman we were left with – because she was no relation – used to tell us we had been left because we were so tiresome and she had taken us in out of pity; but in a desperate moment Ruddy questioned her husband and he said that was only 'Aunty's' fun, and Papa had left us to be taken care of because India was too hot for small people. But we knew better; we had been to Nassick, the Hill Station of Bombay. So what could be the real reason? We couldn't think – and it worried us terribly.

I wonder if psychoanalysts are correct in their claim that early

* *Kipling Journal*, XIV (Dec 1947) 3–5.

influences can poison or seriously overshadow later life. According to their gloomy theories my brother should have grown up morbid, misanthropic, narrow-minded, self-centred, shunning the world and bearing all men a burning grudge. Whereas, of course, he was just the opposite. Certainly between the ages of six and eleven, he was thwarted at every turn and inhibitions were his daily bread. I was rather spoilt – before I saw through 'Aunty' – but Ruddy was systematically bullied day and night. I think 'Aunty's' very worst defect was her unceasing desire to weaken the affection between the poor little people marooned on the desert island of her house and heart. She took the line that I was always in the right and Ruddy always in the wrong – a very alienating position to thrust me into, but he never loved me the less for her mischief-making. There could hardly have been a more miserable childhood.

However, we amused ourselves together. We had a sort of play that ran on and on for months, in which we played all the parts. I'm afraid there was generally a murder in it; or we ran away to sea and had the most wonderful adventures. *I* was the reader in those days, funnily enough, because I had more time as I didn't go to school. I remember *telling* Ruddy *David Copperfield* which I much preferred to *Ministering Children*.[1] It was strange, but Ruddy only learned to read with the greatest difficulty; I think, because he was too clever. I've noticed it with other clever children. A clever child will listen as long as you like while you read to him but can't be bothered with 'A fat cat sat on the mat.' Now I was interested in the fat cat and wanted to follow up its story. I remember a thing Ruddy said to me quite seriously – I must have been four then, because I had been promoted to reading my verse of the psalms at family prayers while Ruddy was still spelling letters into syllables. I was probably crowing over him and he said, 'No, Trix, you're too little you see; you haven't brains enough to understand the hard things about reading. *I* want to know *why* "t" with "hat" after it should be "that".'

In his early days Ruddy was a sturdy little boy in a sailor suit, with long straight fair hair – yes, flaxen fair – eyes like dark violets and a particularly beautiful mouth. He was thoroughly happy and genial – indeed, rather noisy and spoilt. Mother used to say that, like Kim, he was 'Little friend of all the world' and that's what the Indian servants in Bombay called him before we came home. Shyness and Ruddy were never in the same room; *I* was shy, but he always spoke for both of us. He always looked upon me as a fairy gift, and he never resented my coming as some little boys would have done. When people asked him in Bombay, 'Is that your sister?' he would say, 'No, that is my *lady*.'

When Ruddy was thirteen and I was eleven he went to school at Westward Ho!, and I lived with mother in London. She had come home hotfoot from India because Ruddy's eyes had got so bad that a doctor had written to her about them. I remember how at that time we all had a lovely holiday at a farm in Epping Forest; I don't know how mother survived it, we were so absolutely lawless and unchecked. Our cousin Stanley Baldwin came for a six-week visit and we infected him with our lawlessness too – even to donkey-riding. He brought a bat and tried to teach us cricket, but we had no time for it – it entailed too much law and order.

Then, before he was seventeen, Ruddy went off to work in India; I was left behind with three kind old ladies in Warwick Gardens.[2] I should tell you that, for a while, Ruddy had a fancy to be a doctor; I think he regarded it from the noble point of view as an ideal profession. But a wise friend of our aunt's took him to a post-mortem. Ruddy never described it to me; all he said was, 'Oh, Infant' – I had become 'Infant' by then, not 'Trix' – 'Oh, Infant, Mark Twain had a word for it.' Dramatic pause. 'I believe I threw up my immortal soul.' He threw up, anyway, the idea of doctoring. He was writing verses like anything by this time.

Funnily enough, just at the time when most boys cast off home life, Ruddy returned to it like a duck to its pond. I really believe that the happiest time of his life – and mine – was when we all lived together after I came out to Lahore. He was eighteen then and I was fifteen. Although Ruddy and I were always devoted comrades there was never any Charles-and-Mary-Lamb or Dorothy-and-William-Wordsworth nonsense about us. We were each going to live our own lives in our own way; he wasn't going to devote himself to nursing my grey hairs or anything of that kind. For instance, there was a man who wanted to marry me – a lifelong friend of Ruddy's – and he kept on writing me letters. I took one of them to Ruddy one day and said, 'Here's Herbert again; what *am* I to do?' Ruddy shifted his pipe to the other side of his mouth and said, 'Shoot the brute!' That was all the help I got from *him*.

By this time, of course, Ruddy was writing with both hands and a pen in his mouth, as mother used to say. Till fountain-pens came in he was a persistent pen-biter; in every room in our house there was a writing table and on every table was a tray of pens and father said he couldn't find a pen that wasn't bitten into a faggot at the end. So he took to dipping them in quassia.[3] Ruddy always discussed things with me, and I can still recognise 'something of myself' in his writing – in *Departmental Ditties* especially. Mother and I used to drop severely on things his women said in *Plain Tales*. 'No, Ruddy, no! Not that.' 'But it's true.' 'Never mind; there are lots of things that are true that we never mention.' . . . Yes, I think, that was the happiest time in both our lives.

NOTES

1. This book, by Maria Louisa Charlesworth (1819–80), bore the subtitle 'A Tale Dedicated to Childhood'. Published in 1854, it eventually sold more than 100,000 copies.
2. Off the High Street, Kensington. Named after the Earls of Warwick, the former owners of Holland House, London.
3. Quassia, a drug extracted from the wood of certain tropical American trees, was used in medicine as a bitter tonic, as a remedy for threadworms in children, and as an insecticide.

My Brother, Rudyard Kipling (2)*

ALICE MACDONALD FLEMING

Ruddy's success in India was doled out drop by drop; people said, 'Clever young pup!' and talked about his awful side. But in London success came as a flood. It amazed him; he couldn't understand it. He never got a swelled head in the least, even when he received letters – extraordinary letters – from quite cultivated women who wanted to marry him, on or without sight. He came in for a fearfully foggy winter in London and he didn't like it one little bit. When I came 'home' I went to see him in Embankment Chambers,[1] now called 'Kipling House' – and he was very *piano*[2] and longing for the parents again. It was then that he sent a telegram to father in India;

* *Kipling Journal*, XIV (Apr 1948) 7–8.

it just said, 'Genesis 45: 9.' But that verse reads – and do please remember that Ruddy's first name was 'Joseph' – 'Haste ye and go up to my father and say unto him, Thus sayeth thy son Joseph, God hath made me lord of all Egypt; come down unto me, tarry not . . . ' The parents *did* come down to Egypt and for a while we had a charming house in Earl's Court Road. That was the time when Ruddy was writing 'The Flag of England' and he was stuck at the very first line, and he said to mother, 'What am I trying to say?' and mother said, quick as a flash, 'What do they know of England who only England know?' . . . I think it's characteristic of Ruddy that two of his best known lines were written by his mother; the other one is 'East is East and West is West and never the twain shall meet.'

He loved going about and seeing things; he was always observing; he had a camera in his brain. He liked going to the docks – Limehouse and so on – and he had the golden gift of making everybody talk to him. He didn't care for games and he didn't go out much. He had strong dislikes; he couldn't stand goody-goods, for instance. But it is not true that he detested cats, though two months after his death a well-known Sunday paper announced with what Shelley calls 'the natural glee of a wolf that has smelt out a dead child', that 'Kipling had always hated cats to the verge of cruelty and beyond it.' If anyone can prove to me that my brother hated or was deliberately cruel to any animal, I will kill that animal with my own hands and eat it raw! He was devoted to all nature and never owned a gun.

Ruddy always had an idea – it strengthened, I'm afraid, in later days – that people were trying to pick his brains; he became therefore very cautious. People were always wanting introductions and their stupid little stories written for them and so on. He very much enjoyed theatres and people said he should have gone on the stage; he was a curiously good character-actor. He used to get the most extraordinary mail in London from quite well-known names; one very distinguished writer and critic wrote – on exquisite deckle-edged parchment – to thank 'one so young and yet a Master' for 'feeding him the True Bread and Wine of the Word'. Ruddy's scribbled footnote was, 'The old josser means *Soldiers Three*.'

About his writing he always said to the last, 'I shall write something worth reading one day.' I don't think he was specially pleased with anything that he had done. He liked *Kim* and the Jungle Books, but the silliest little limerick he wrote would delight him – for the moment – as much as the most serious poem. Luckily the mere physical act of writing was a pleasure to him; he loved it. He was never a note-taker; he drew hieroglyphics – doodles and little funny pictures were his form of note-taking.

I am afraid you will say that I have been telling you too much about my brother's youth, but as I said at the beginning, that is the part of him I find myself going back to. *I* married in 1889 and *he* married three years later, and after that, our paths in the world divided. He went west and I went east, and the personal devil seemed to arrange that seldom the twain should meet; at any rate, our leaves in England very rarely coincided. But we wrote to each other a lot and we never lost our pleasure in exchanging the apt quotation. If he could hear me now – and, you know, I believe he *is* hearing me – I think he would appreciate this couplet from George Eliot:

> But could another childhood be my share
> I would be born a little sister there.

NOTES

1. Kipling lived on Villiers Street, Charing Cross, while writing *The Light that Failed*.
2. A soft, low tone, lacking in vigour or power.

As a Tale that Is Told: Recollections of Many Years*

FREDERIC W. MACDONALD

Towards the end of May 1891, I received a most affecting letter from my brother in New York. He told me that for some time he had been very unwell, that his ailment was now discovered to be

* (London, New York, Toronto and Melbourne: Cassell, 1919) pp. 199–200.

incurable, and that he had not long to live. 'My first thought', said he, 'was that I would at once wind up my affairs here and come with my wife to England that I might see you all once more, die among my own people, and be laid by my father and mother. But my doctors tell me that I should not survive the voyage, but be buried in the Atlantic. So, if it is at all possible, come at once, my dear brother, and see me for the last time.' I was, as may be supposed, greatly distressed, but immediately made the necessary arrangements and secured my passage.

My nephew, Mr Rudyard Kipling, being at the time a good deal out of health, determined upon a voyage to New York and back, and we sailed together from Liverpool. With a view to maintaining his privacy and being spared the fatigue and excitement of company, he also registered under the name of Macdonald. In a few days, however, his health and spirits were so far restored that he began to mingle with his fellow-passengers, and the qualities of his conversation led one and another of the more knowing to make a good guess at his personality. But both he and I, when questioned on the subject, to use the words of Tennyson, 'smiled, and put the question by'. We had scarcely reached our hotel in New York when the rumour that Mr Kipling, under the name of Macdonald, had just landed brought down upon us the enterprising interviewer. He inquired for Mr Macdonald, and I received him. Approaching me with a particularly intelligent smile, as of one who had got hold of the right end of a secret, he said, 'Mr Kipling, I believe.' I told him he was mistaken; that my name was Macdonald. Finding him incredulous and persistent, I admitted that Mr Kipling was with me, but was unwell, and had made up his mind not to receive callers or be interviewed by the Press. To this I held in spite of all his blandishments, and he finally departed in sorrow and in anger. To the latter, I imagine, was due the statement in next morning's paper that Mr Kipling had arrived in New York, but was a wreck in body and mind.

NOTE

The Revd Frederic Macdonald (1842–1928) was the son of the Revd George Browne Macdonald (1805–68) and his wife Hannah (1809–75). His sister Georgiana married Sir Edward Burne-Jones, the famous artist. He introduced their sister Alice (1837–1910) to John Lockwood Kipling (1837–1911), and they married on 18 March 1865. A liberal Wesleyan minister who became in 1899 President of the Methodist Conference, Rudyard's uncle had an active ministry from 1862 to 1928.

Some Memories of my Cousin*

FLORENCE MACDONALD

It has been truly said, 'Memory is a crazy witch, she treasures bits of rag and straw, and throws her jewels out of the window', so doubtless many of my jewels are lost, and I can only give you the fragments – very precious to me – which remain.

No one will be surprised to hear that Rudyard Kipling was remarkable from his earliest years; and, apropos of his first visit to our home when he was about four years of age, my father described him in a letter as a 'formidable element in the home', which one can readily believe. At the age of six months his mother wrote of him: 'He notices everything he sees, and when he is not sitting up in his ayah's arms, he turns round to follow things with his eyes very comically.' Of his sister, when a little under two, she wrote, 'She develops a talent for apposite quotation'; while Ruddy, aged four, was perplexing himself with abstruse subjects, and said one day, 'I can't imagine what God made me of. It can't be dust, because there's red blood inside me!'

But my memories begin when he was about twelve years of age and sometimes joined our family circle for his holidays, when his coming was hailed with joy by us children, but perhaps with less enthusiasm by our mother who had already six of her own; he was several years older than we were, and a precocious boy at that; with insatiable curiosity and exhaustless enterprise, he often led the whole party of us into trouble. But we in the nursery found him a delightful playfellow and story-teller, always full of enthusiasm and new ideas. I remember an occasion when he had his ears boxed by a railway porter for impudence, and he returned to our house swelling with rage and mortification. He stormed up and down the place,

---

* *Kipling Journal*, no. 46 (July 1938) 45–50.

telling us all about it, then pulled himself together and returned to Addison Road Station to repeat the offence.

After those days our lives lay apart – his, at school, in India, America and other places; and with the exception of a few occasions when we met at family gatherings, I did not see much of him, till in his early married life I paid a memorable visit to his home in Devonshire. I was somewhat young for my years, unsophisticated and impressionable, and I shall never forget, and shall always be thankful for, his influence on me in those days. He possessed the charm of making one feel that he was interested in everything one said or thought or did. He was never bored and would kindly encourage, or (should occasion require) gently rebuke. I always felt that he had the qualities of a seer, for, with his inspired insight, he seemed to get beneath the surface and bring to light the real man or woman – not for merciless dissection, but to show the hidden good, the unsuspected valour, or the tremulous fear, and to meet it with a sympathetic understanding which was bracing, not relaxing, in its influence.

It was a tremendous privilege for a girl to have such a friend, and he taught me some valuable lessons. There has been no one in my life to whom I could speak as frankly and as openly as I did to him. We discussed everything – religion, love, politics, sex, and he gave me many wise aphorisms with regard to the conduct of life in general. Once when I was suffering from a long period of ill health he commended me for keeping what he called 'a stiff upper lip', and that encouraging expression has helped me through many a '*mauvais quart d'heure*' ever since.

There is no doubt that he understood the working of a woman's mind. His mother once told me that someone said to her, 'What a lot you must have taught your son about women.' 'On the contrary,' replied my aunt; 'what a lot my son has taught me.' I remember a salutary hour when he looked through some of my own attempts at verse – kindly but firmly criticising, deleting here, putting in there – showing faults of metre and scansion. In one case he crushed me by saying, 'Not a good line in it, my dear', and while I was feeling like drowning myself he lifted me up to a seventh heaven by picking up another, and exclaiming, 'But this is damned good.' Then he told me that if I slogged at it, so many hours a day, regularly, for years, I might some day write good verse, adding, 'You see, there's ink in the blood of the Macdonalds.'

I never heard him say a bitter or harsh word of any other writer, though I do remember when Barrie published *Margaret Ogilvy*,[1] which was supposed to be the story of his mother, he expressed surprise that anyone could make 'copy' of such a sacred thing as his mother.

And what a variety of subjects he could talk about! His knowledge was encyclopaedic, his memory phenomenal – and it was at your service, not as from a patronising pedant, but just as something naturally to be shared with you. I have walked over the Sussex Downs with him while he talked as the spirit moved him, sometimes reciting his latest poems to me, or outlining a story. I have tramped the Devon lanes with him in February, on his eager quest for signs of spring, his whole being thrilled with promise of beauty. Walking near his Sussex estate he would point out to me the various places associated with his *Puck* stories, narrating the incidents so vividly that I expected to meet the characters at every turn of the road. Only two years before his death he pointed out to me a scar on the hillside into which he longed to dig, as he expected to find traces of the forges when Sussex was a land of iron foundries in the days of long ago. And he showed me the mill-stream which served the mill that was named in the Domesday Book.

And how quickly he could change from being the philosopher and historian, and become a rare playfellow. Once, in crossing a field we found a little brook, he quickly made a paper boat, and with sticks to guide it, we two grown-ups had a merry half-hour.

His love of children was a very marked trait in his character: on our walks he would speak to every child he met, or take me into cottages to introduce me to some plump babe. It was a fascinating sight to see him play with a child, for he became a child himself, looking at the game from a child's point of view. I was peremptorily dismissed from the game as too grown-up. I remember when he was a schoolboy how fascinated he was with a tiny babe in our home. He would sit by the cradle holding the little hand in his own grimy paw, and he wrote in a letter at that time that he thought a baby the 'prettiest thing in the world'. How well he understood a child's point of view is evidenced in his *Just So Stories*, where he anticipates just the kind of questions a child would ask, and in his illustrations he puts in all the details that a child would expect to find there. I had the pleasure of hearing him tell these tales to children, an unforgettable experience, each phrase having its special intonation or emphasis.

Everyone realises his love and understanding of animals as shown in his writings, *The Jungle Book* introducing us to a world of creatures that thought, felt, and reasoned like human beings, and no one can read his dog stories and poems without seeing what a special love he had for them. His own dogs were real companions, and he knew what it meant to 'give your heart to a dog to tear'. No one in his estate was allowed to use a gun, and when the wild rabbits became too numerous he saw to it that they were netted and painlessly destroyed.

On occasions I was privileged to sit in his study while he was working – careful not to speak unless I was spoken to. He was very methodical, working for fixed hours each day, not merely waiting till the spirit moved him. He kept plodding at it, whatever his mood. He wrote and rewrote his chapters with great care, deleting here or adding there; nothing careless or slovenly allowed to remain. His amazing detailed knowledge of everything he wrote about is well known; but perhaps it is not always realised what infinite pains he took to acquire exactness. I was staying with him when he was correcting the proofs of *Captains Courageous*, and he showed me a pile of Blue Books which he had gone through in order to assimilate facts about the cod-fisheries of Newfoundland. Another time, when he was writing *Stalky & Co.*, he kept going into fits of laughter, and then he would read to me what he had written and we would laugh together. 'No one', he said, 'gets more fun out of my stories than I do.' Then returning to his desk, having relighted his pipe, he added, 'And now what *shall* we make them do?' When composing verse he would often set it to a tune, usually to a hymn-tune, and I have heard him walking up and down the room singing a verse over and over again in order to get the lilt and swing of it. Sometimes he would ask me to sing some poem to a hymn tune that he suggested – for instance 'McAndrew's Hymn' to 'The Church's One Foundation',[2] or the 'Recessional' to the tune 'For Those in Peril on the Sea'.[3] I also remember at the time of the Boer War singing the 'Absent-minded Beggar'[4] to him as we walked over the Downs behind Rottingdean. And he told me that he had said to Sir Arthur Sullivan recently, who set the words to music, 'You and I ought to have been shot for perpetrating such stuff', but he added to me, 'But it did the job, it brought in the pennies.'

He had a great shrinking from publicity, and shunned everything in the way of social lionising. In his younger days he was really very naughty about it – parties were arranged in his honour, to which the elite of the land were invited, and when the day arrived the 'lion' never turned up. I have heard of distracted hostesses with a drawing-room full of guests eager to meet him, but RK had disappeared, only to be discovered later, sitting on the nursery floor with the children tumbling about him. His home at Rottingdean was made impossible to him owing to the vulgar curiosity of sightseers who would arrive in charabancs, and congregate round the gate of his house, which in self defence he had to have boarded up to ensure any privacy; and even then they would peer through the hole necessary for the latch of the gate, in hopes of a glimpse of the celebrated author. His Burwash house lay off the beaten track – a beautiful Elizabethan house hidden in a hollow, and there he sought and found privacy and quiet.

I remember, when he was at the zenith of his fame, being much struck by his humility about his gifts. I foolishly said that I wondered he wasn't made conceited by the adulations that were showered on him, and he replied, 'But why? It is nothing to do with me; it is something put into me from outside. I am but the humble instrument, and it's a grand responsibility.' He has expressed this idea in one of his verses:

> If there be good in that I wrought
> Thy Hand compelled it, Master, Thine –
> Where I have failed to meet Thy Thought
> I know, through Thee, the blame is mine.

There was a deep religious strain in him, though he seldom attended public worship, or spoke on religious matters, but one was aware of it in his attitude to life and his general outlook, and it was very evident in some of his writings, especially in his verse, such as 'Recessional', or 'The Children's Hymn', etc. With regard to the former, he remarked to my father after its publication that when one has three generations of Methody ministers behind one, the pulpit streak is bound to show.

There may be some here who do not know that Rudyard was a grandson of the Manse on both sides – his paternal grandfather being the Revd Joseph Kipling, and his maternal grandfather the Revd George Browne Macdonald, both Wesleyan ministers. And now my memories have come to an end it is a melancholy thought that there is no chance of their being increased, but such as they are I share them with you, in a spirit of love and loyalty to one whom this Society delights to honour, and whom I have the privilege to claim as my kinsman and very dear friend.

NOTES

Florence Macdonald was daughter of the Revd Frederic Macdonald (1842–1928) and Mary Cork (d. 1909); Rudyard Kipling's cousin.

1. Sir James Matthew Barrie (1860–1937) published the poignant story of the life and death of his mother, *Margaret Ogilvy*, in 1896.

2. Music by S. S. Wesley, words by S. J. Stone, written in 1866. Stone was moved to the composition of this hymn by his admiration of a Cape Town bishop (Gray) who defended the Catholic faith against the teachings of Bishop Colenso. When all the bishops assembled for the Lambeth Conference (1888), this hymn was chosen as the processional for the services at Canterbury Cathedral, Westminster Abbey and St Paul's Cathedral.

3. Music by William Whiting (1860), words by John B. Dykes (1861). Often known by its first line, 'Eternal Father, strong to save', and the rest of the stanza: 'Whose arm doth bind the restless wave, Who bidd'st the mighty ocean deep/Its own appointed limits keep', followed by the refrain, 'Oh hear us when we cry to thee/For those in peril on the sea.'

4. A recruiting poem written during the early period of the Boer War Extraordinarily popular after its first publication in the *Daily Mail* (Oct 1899), the poem raised over 250,000 pounds for soldiers' dependants. Sir Arthur Sullivan, in Kipling's vivid phrase, 'wedded the words to a tune guaranteed to pull teeth out of barrel-organs'.

Part II
Westward Ho!

Kipling at School*

MICHAEL GIFFORD WHITE

It is generally conceded that in the lives of all men who rise to great distinction the influences which are brought to bear upon them during their earlier years leave marks which are never effaced, that in the boy is to be discerned much of the forthcoming man.

As in the case of Charles Dickens this appears also, in a measure, to be that of the foremost literary man of the end of the century, Rudyard Kipling, who was better known to the writer as simply 'Gigs' – Gigs the irrepressible fellow, always in some harmless mischief, always playing off some joke upon either one of the masters or his schoolfellows, no respecter of persons, and not caring one jot what good or evil opinion those held of him with whom he came in daily contact.

And this trend of disposition was certainly inclined to be fostered by the environment in which Kipling found himself at the United Service College, Westward Ho!,[1] during the six or seven years between the time he left India as a child and returned to that country almost a man. . . .

It is a coincidence, worthy of notice to those parents whose children are not, perhaps, so devoted to their books as might seem desirable, that not only Kipling but both his chosen companions evinced little ambition to stand at the head of a class. The whole world is aware of the pedestal upon which one of the three now stands, but it may be interesting also to call to mind the fact that the other two, when the time came, passed brilliantly into the scientific branch of the British military service.

As an illustration of Kipling's behaviour in class, there was a certain geography master who greatly favoured the drawing of sections of the earth's surface, showing the mountain-ranges, rivers, lakes, seas, strata, etc., which were generally executed by his pupils on sheets of foolscap.

* *Independent* (New York) LI (16 Mar 1899) 752–4.

At first the master was contented with quite ordinary distances between two given points, as from London to Edinburgh, Paris to Berlin, and so forth; but gradually he came to lengthen them out to an alarming extent – Chicago to Timbuctoo, Vladivostok to Goa, Cape Town to Moscow, which, while it embarrassed the rest of the boys, suggested a humorous idea to Kipling.

From somewhere or other he procured several rolls of wallpaper, and then day and night with pens and brushes he laboured diligently on a gigantic section, inserting men, birds, beasts and fishes, trees – in fact, anything he could think of, which being at length completed to his satisfaction, Kipling calmly awaited the result of his joke.

When at last the geographical master called for that particular section, to his surprise and the amusement of Kipling's classmates, Kipling unwound his gigantic roll on the floor. At first it was evident that the master mentally debated the question as to whether it was a case demanding a public rebuke by the instant use of the cane, or commendation in its highest form by full marks, when Kipling's absolutely innocent expression of countenance decided him to adopt the latter course.

The English public-school system of fagging was established at Westward Ho! in two forms, study fagging and fagging at games. In the first case a lower-school boy was attached to prefect or sub-prefect to attend to his study, cook his breakfast and tea, and run his errands, for the space of a term. The second form was a daily list of the names of small boys, posted by the captains of games, whose task it was to tug a huge roller over the cricket or tennis lawns, or to field the balls for the practice of the first eleven. Kipling, for some reason, escaped the former service, but his name was often down in the latter list. He never rose sufficiently high in the school to possess a fag of his own.

At the end of his college career Kipling left Westward Ho! in the ordinary manner, and not, as has been recently stated, as a 'runaway truant', having gained, in spite of his pranks and peculiar humours, the regard of his masters and schoolfellows, the general opinion being that he was an awfully clever chap – was 'Gigs'.

NOTE

Michael White, a schoolmate at Westward Ho!, occupied the study below that of Kipling, and had the singular honour of having 'fried bacon fat' poured on his head by Kipling. The two remained friends nevertheless.

1. This school, established for the main purpose of training the children of military personnel to compete successfully in civil service examinations, was named after a place in the fiction of Charles Kingsley (1819–75). It was located in a small seaside village near Barnstaple, Devon.

Stalky's Reminiscences*

L. C. DUNSTERVILLE

I cannot remember exactly when Kipling or Beresford came to the school, but I suppose it was in my third year, which would be about 1878.

We eventually shared a study together, but must have formed our first alliance long before that time. The greater part of our 'study' period was passed together, but not all. There were changes in the combination at one time or another, the details of which I cannot recall.

From the details I have given of my life up to this point, it will be realised that I had gained some considerable experience, and had probably a good deal of skill in manoeuvre, coupled with other traits that might give promising results when combined with the precociously mature mentality of Kipling and the subtle ingenuity of Beresford.

I am sure we were not posing, and we were not setting out merely to defy authority, but almost unconsciously I am afraid that was our attitude. We must have been heartily disliked by both masters and senior boys – and with entire justification.

The first effect the combination had on me was to improve my taste in literature. The period of Ned Kelly[1] and Jack Harkaway[2] was succeeded by Ruskin, Carlyle, and Walt Whitman.

We did a good deal of reading, hidden away in our hut in the middle of the densest patch of furze-bushes, or in a tiny room we hired from one of the cottagers. Our various huts were mostly 'out of bounds', but the secret entrance to them was sometimes in bounds,

---

* (London: Jonathan Cape, 1928) pp. 43–7, 49–51, 56.

in which case one ran no risk of capture on entering or leaving. And capture in the hut itself was practically impossible. The furze-thicket was on a steep slope, the tunnel of approach between the prickly stems of the bushes was only just wide enough to admit a boy. A grown-up endeavouring to approach from above could only do so (as we did) by pushing through the furze-bushes and moving down backwards. Progress in this way was slow, and grunts and exclamations when contact was obtained with healthy furze-prickles gave notice long before the danger could be at all acute.

Approached from below, things were easier, but for that reason we never made our main road in that direction; the little track there was only an emergency exit and quite impossible for a full-sized man to negotiate.

The joy of a hut was manifold. It was out of bounds; it was one spot in the world out of reach of grown-ups. Then there was the joy of construction. Finally, there was the joy of smoking, often ending in the misery of being sick. Reading to ourselves or out loud was our only recreation, and the hatching of plots against people who had 'incurred our odium'. *The Confessions of a Thug*[3] was one of the books we read aloud, and Walt Whitman we thoroughly enjoyed in the same way. You can't get the real effect out of WW in any other way. *Fors Clavigera*[4] and *Sartor Resartus*[5] and other works we absorbed in silence, broken only by occasional comments.

I can't remember why on earth we hired that little room from 'Rabbit's-eggs', but I suppose it was in the winter and our outdoor haunts were damp and uncomfortable. I call it a room but I fancy it must really have been something more in the nature of a pigsty. But whatever it was, we cleaned it up and had the same joy in its occupancy as we had in our hut – the feeling of security and escape from tyranny. We did some cooking over a methylated spirit-lamp – the usual brews of cocoa and tea, and occasional odds and ends that a kindly fate had put in our way on our travels.

Old Gregory, from whom we hired this room, was a rather dull-witted peasant who was frequently under the influence of drink. His nickname of 'Rabbit's-eggs' was due to his having offered for sale six partridge eggs which he stoutly maintained were 'rabbut's aigs'. He genuinely believed them to be so. He was passing a clump of bushes when a rabbit ran out of them and for some reason or another he peered into the bushes, and there, sure enough, were the six eggs, obviously the produce of the rabbit!

He was inclined to be quarrelsome in his cups and possessed a dreadful vocabulary of the very worst expletives, which gave rise to his secondary nickname of 'Scoffer'. These were traits that could obviously be used to advantage if handled judiciously.

We were given the privilege of a study about 1880. It was conceded to us rather reluctantly, though, as a matter of fact, we were just the sort of people who could get the greatest advantage out of such a privilege.

We took great pains over the aesthetic adornment of our study, the scheme being based on olive-green, and some grey-blue paint with which we did some remarkable stencilling. Curio shops at Bideford furnished us with quaint fragments of old oak-carving, ancient prints, and some good, but damaged, pieces of old china.

Finance was difficult. We were none of us very plentifully supplied with funds, and after the first month of term bankruptcy generally stared us in the face. On emergency the sale of a suit of clothes filled the gap, and we devised many similar expedients to tide us over a bad time.

At our most severe crisis, when the larder was quite empty, I made a useful discovery. In playing about with the fire I found by chance that used tea-leaves placed on a hot shovel crinkle back into their original shapes and look as if they had never been used. It was easy to turn this discovery to our immediate advantage. I did up about half a pound of tea-leaves in this way and put them back into their original package. Then I visited the study below and exchanged them for about half the proper tea-value of cocoa.

They returned the tea with threats on the following day, but in the meantime we had swallowed the cocoa. Peace was restored by our confession and an offer to regard the cocoa as a loan to be repaid when funds were available.

We did not spend much of our money on tobacco, because our smoking was really more bravado than pleasure. A clay pipe and an ounce of shag last a very long time. During one term we revelled in big cigars, or they revelled in us. We made constant efforts to smoke one to the end, but the attempt was either abandoned or ended in disaster. . . .

The Natural History Society,[6] founded by Mr Evans in 1880, soon attracted our attention, and I think we all three became members. It was not so much the pursuit of butterflies, or the study of birds and plants, that drew us to the Society as the valuable privileges conferred on members, the chief of which was a relaxation of bounds. Places that we could only visit hitherto by stealth we could now walk boldly through, carrying in our hands some hastily-gathered botanical specimens or matchboxes containing beetles or caterpillars. With these we could smilingly confront the sergeant or any prowling master who had 'stalked' us with a view to punishment for breaking bounds.

But one's nature cannot be wholly evil, and a small spark of something good in mine was fired by Evans' enthusiasm for botany. I interested myself in flowers merely in order to carry out nefarious schemes with greater impunity, but I ended in loving flowers for their own sakes. My slight knowledge of botany has been a source of pleasure to me all of my life.

The Literary and Debating Society attracted us in a more genuine way and we extracted quite a lot of amusement out of it. Kipling was made Editor of the school *Chronicle*, and some of his earliest efforts appeared in that paper. I remember 'Ave Imperatrix',[7] written in the style of a poet-laureate congratulating a monarch on escape from peril. This was with reference to an attempt on the life of Queen Victoria about 1881. Poets would not be poets if they could know when the divine frenzy was going to inspire them, and when a poet happens to be also a schoolboy the inspiration is pretty certain to come at an unsuitable moment. So it happened that 'Ave Imperatrix' was written in a French class at the end of a French textbook.

Looking back on my own school-days, I am filled with an intense sympathy for schoolmasters. What a wearisome and thankless task is theirs! I regarded them as a tyrannical lot of old men (some probably not more than twenty-six years old) who hated boys and wanted to make them miserable. So I, in my turn, tried to make them miserable. I know better now, and I hope that boys of these days are not so stupid as I was, and have a fairer estimate of the relative positions of master and boy than I had.

Kipling must have been a difficult youth. The ordinary boy, however truculent, generally quails before the malevolent glance of a notably fierce master. But I remember Kipling on such occasions merely removing his glasses, polishing them carefully, replacing them on his nose and gazing in placid bewilderment at the thundering tyrant, with a look that suggested, 'There, there. Don't give way to your little foolish tantrums. Go out and get a little fresh air, and you'll come back feeling quite another man.'

Kipling's sight was a great handicap to him in the knockabout life of boyhood. Without his glasses he was practically blind. We fought occasionally, as the best of friends always do. He was quite muscular, but shorter than me, and this gave me some advantage. But as you cannot fight with specs on, my victory was always an easy affair – taking a mean advantage of an opponent who could not see what he was hitting at.

Like all schools, we had compulsory cricket or football three times a week, but it was foolish to expect a boy with a large pair of specs on his nose to take much interest in the 'scrum' of Rugby football.

Kipling's only nickname at school was 'Giglamps' – sometimes shortened to 'Gigger' – derived from the very strong glasses he was compelled to wear. . . .

The first break-up of our little band was in 1882, when Kipling left for India to take up an appointment with the *Civil and Military Gazette* at Lahore. Beresford left a short time later to join Cooper's Hill Engineering College,[8] whence he also eventually found his way to India, in the Public Works Department; and I left at the end of the summer term 1883, to enter the Royal Military College, Sandhurst.

NOTES

Lionel Charles Dunsterville (1865–1946) served in Waziristan, 1894–5; North-west Frontier, India, 1897–8; in China, 1900; and in the Great War. He wrote *The Adventures of Dunsterforce* (1920), *And Obey?* (1925), *Stalky's Reminiscences* (1928), *More Yarns* (1931), and *Stalky Settles Down* (1932). He was the first president of the Kipling Society, which was founded in 1927.

1. A famous bushranger and Australian rural outlaw in the late 1870s; often thought of as a champion of workers' rights and an enemy of large land-owners; the subject of many stories and books written for children. Edward Kelly (1855–1880) was hanged after a pitched battle with police in New South Wales.

2. The first Jack Harkaway story appeared in *Boys of England*, 23 July 1871. Samuel Bracebridge Hemyng (1841–1901), a barrister and son of the Registrar of the Supreme Court of Calcutta, wrote at least fourteen volumes in this 'penny dreadful' series.

3. Written by Captain Meadows Taylor, and published in 1840.

4. By John Ruskin; published between 1871 and 1884.

5. Written by Thomas Carlyle in 1830–1; published in *Fraser's Magazine*, 1833–4.

6. 'Hartopp' in *Stalky & Co.* (or Mr Evans) was a sympathetic teacher, admired by Kipling, who organised a society to encourage students to pay closer attention to the natural phenomena of Devon. Mr Evans also promoted theatricals.

7. First published in the eighth issue of the *United Services College Chronicle* (1882); reprinted in 'An English School' in *Youth's Companion* (1893), and collected in *Land and Sea Tales* (1923).

8. Cooper's Hill, in Egham, Surrey, achieved fame in Sir John Denham's topographical poem (1642). The Royal Indian Civil Engineering College educated men for the public works, accounts, railways and telegraph departments of India. It closed in 1906.

Stalky's School-days*

L. C. DUNSTERVILLE

I am afraid I have chosen a very well-worn subject about which to talk to you this evening, and I hope you are not all too tired to be interested. I shall give you details of those happy days of boyhood when Kipling, Beresford and myself showed no signs at all of becoming the highly respectable citizens we now are – quite exemplary and beyond reproach. But a word of warning as to these details. I caused great indignation in the breasts of septuagenarians, octogenarians, nonagenarians and centenarians some years ago by an article in which I said that sixty years was a great age. I went on to say that the memories of old gentlemen were not to be trusted! Do not accept any of their statements without triple corroboration. So you see that what I am about to tell you may be pure romance, and I hope that Mr Beresford is in the room to amuse you by contradicting all my 'facts'.

Kipling, however, is more reliable, as he wrote *Stalky & Co.*[1] when he was about thirty-two, before his memory had become blurred. The point of these remarks is this. Kipling and myself had a general agreement in our recollections – though it is natural that certain incidents are more deeply impressed on his mind than mine,

---

* *Kipling Journal*, no. 22 (June 1932) pp. 46–8.

and *vice versa* – the question of saloon pistols, for example. I have not denied many of Beresford's statements yet, because he has not put them down in print. I am waiting till he does so, when I shall be forced to disprove most of his best stories, and our editor may be able to fill many pages of the *Journal* with our acrimonious correspondence – if the subject would interest his readers.

Young people in the room will be amazed to hear that the period under discussion is 1875 to 1883, which will seem to them almost like another era. I will start with a few remarks about the book *Stalky & Co*. It has been very widely read in England and America, and I find that most readers make two great mistakes. In the first place they seem to forget that Kipling is a writer of fiction and not of history, and in the second place some of them seem to believe that it was his intention to give a typical picture of public-school life in general.

I have suffered a good deal from the first error. I have been identified with 'Stalky', and have to accept the praise or blame attached by the reader to that character. I have met people who, assuming me to possess the astuteness and ability of Stalky, have placed me on a pedestal far above my merits. They have been bitterly disappointed at my not giving an immediate display of my supposed talents. On the other hand an old lady friend wrote to me not long ago, 'I have read *Stalky & Co.*, I wish I had not!'

It must be remembered that neither Kipling nor I have ever stated that I was Stalky. My own recollection of myself (which may be faulty!) is that of a nice clean little boy, always spotlessly turned out, and with his hair parted neatly in the middle, who was always an example to the race of schoolboys, and who failed for seven and a half weary years to receive the prize for good conduct owing to circumstances over which he had no control.

The truth of the matter is this. Kipling, Beresford and myself were closely associated during our school careers and, in the later years, shared a study and a common purse. The incidents recorded in the book are of the nature of actual incidents, but cannot be regarded as history. The later life of Stalky is on the lines of my own experience serving with the Sikhs, Dogras[2] and Pathans[3] on the North-west Frontier of India, where the barren mountains of the Suleiman Range separate an ordinary civilisation from the haunts of the fierce and independent Pathans; but the heroic episodes of that portion of the book may be taken with a whole cellar-full of salt. The picture is realistic, but the incidents are either purely imaginary or collected from various sources.

To return to the 'traditional' characters of the book. It is quite true that we three were leagued together in every sort of evil-doing, though I hope our 'evil' may have been tempered with what appeared to our youthful minds to be a feeling of justice, and the sketches of character are not untrue to life. I will ask you to consider as strictly true all the incidents that you consider exhibit the better traits, and as pure fiction anything you don't like about the trio. It is certain that none of the three were quite normal boys, and that the actual three did not make themselves quite as obnoxious to both masters and boys as the three characters in the book.

Admitting, then, that the three characters of Beetle, M'Turk and Stalky are based upon the individualities of Kipling, Beresford and myself, I will tell you that we were not successful in all our enterprises, and I might almost add that I bear on my back the proofs of this assertion – the honourable scars of war! Certainly I bore no grudge against the beater, whether master or prefect, feeling a secret exultation in the thought that if I was getting six for a crime discovered, I was escaping fifty-six overdue for undiscovered breaches of the law.

As regards the question of Kipling's intention to hand down to posterity a true picture of normal boys' life in a normal school, no careful reader could make such an assumption. The clear facts are that the boys were not normal boys, the masters (though in many cases highly gifted) were not normal masters, and the school in general was not of a normal type.

NOTES

1. Published by Macmillan in 1899.

2. A race of Hill Rajputs in India, inhabiting Kashmir and the adjacent villages of the Himalayas. 'Dogra' denotes the country around Jammu. Its people, irrespective of religion or caste, are called Dogras.

3. A name applied throughout India to the Afghans, especially to those settled in the country and to those dwelling on the borderland.

School-days with Kipling*

GEORGE CHARLES BERESFORD

Into the small-boys' house at Westward Ho! in the gray, chill
January days of 1878 there fluttered a cheery, capering, podgy,
little fellow, as precocious as ever he could be. Or, rather, a broad
smile appeared with a small boy behind it, carrying it about and
pointing it in all directions. On persistent inquiry the name of the
smile turned out to be 'Kipling' – only that and nothing more: a
modest name, almost diminutive, for such a broad smile and such a
podgy person. Over the smile there was strangely enough, a pair of
spectacles. The two did not quite seem to go together, as in those
days spectacles were regarded as a mark of extreme seriousness and
crabbed age. Later, we got quite accustomed to the combination
and thought they agreed.

When you looked more closely at this new boy, you were
astonished to see what seemed to be a moustache right across the
smile; and so it was – an early spring moustache just out of the
ground of his upper lip. Kipling's hair being dark, the moustache
was visible, when you really had twigged it was a moustache, from
quite a number of feet off. It was not actually against regulations for
lower schoolboys to wear moustaches, but it looked like trespassing
on the privileges of the prefects and the upper sixth, who could – if
able and so disposed – display some faint pencilling on the upper lip.
However, it was not advisable to order the new arrival to shave, so
the matter was passed over.

Kipling was rather short for his age of just twelve years; but he
took it out in extra width. He was not noticeably muscular or
sinewy, and was accordingly ineffectual at fisticuffs, for which, in
any case, his exceedingly short sight unfitted him. He preferred to
side-track physical violence by his tact and friendliness and by not
quarrelling with any boy unless he had allies. He was always

* (New York: G. P. Putnam's Sons, 1936) pp. 1–6, 12–15, 60–2, 103–9, 167–
176.

noticeable for his caution and his habit of 'getting there' by diplomatic methods.

The modelling of his head was peculiar. His skull appeared of moderate size in relation to his rather large face; his forehead reteated sharply from a heavy browline – in fact, so sharp was the set-back from the massive eyebrow ridges that he appeared almost 'cave-boy'. His lower jaw was massive, protruding and strong; the chin had a deep central cleft or dimple that at once attracted attention. Owing to its width, his face appeared rather Mongolian, and, bar the specs, he looked rather more formidable than he was. His complexion was dark rather than pale; the darkish hair was always close cropped.

His mouth was wide, with very well shaped lips that suggested song – a promise that actuality denied. His hands and fingers were small. The short neck was set on rather round shoulders. He had a very slight stoop and a slightly round back that would be unpleasing to a sergeant-major. The curve in the shoulder region and an apparently small head close to the shoulders earned him the nickname of 'The Beetle'; but this appellation was current only amongst a few, although used throughout in *Stalky & Co.*

The spectacles of the new boy that attracted so much notice consisted of pebble lenses framed in dark blue steel. These glasses, of course, had to be carefully inspected by the boys, and it was explained to them that glass lenses were too easily scratched in wiping and that there was some further matter of better refraction. At any rate, the pebbles stayed the course till they were broken. The eyes without their glassy dress were strange, vibrating and blind, only seeing clearly a matter of inches. When reading, which Kipling always did without his specs, they were in constant movement, jiggering about till again safely behind their armour of pebble.

As Kipling was the only boy in the school wearing glasses, he required a nickname to emphasise the peculiarity. What it should be was in doubt for quite time. The honour of finally giving the right and inevitable appellation falls not to the school, with all its learning, but to a member of the bucolic *entourage*, a vendor of some sort of supplies, or the laundry-cart man who, seeing our hero among a small crowd of boys, asked, 'Who's they old Giglamps?'

The name was immediately adopted with acclamation; but for everyday use it shortened to 'Gigs' or 'Gigger'.

Gigger, as he will henceforth be dubbed in this narrative, was, behind his smile, his moustache and his giglamps, in manner ingratiating and tactful, meeting all remarks derogatory or otherwise with a smile and parrying more direct attacks with a rapidly conceived jest; so much so that the little boys of Prout's house, where Gigger had come to anchor, forgot to be disagreeable, and, after saying, 'What is your name?' and receiving the surname straight and square, without frills or Christian names, rather quieted down, trying to digest this combination of smile, specs and moustache.

There was laughter wherever Gigger was – out of school hours. He was regarded as our greatest acquisition, the most amusing piece of apparatus we possessed in the bleak form-room that was the sole abiding-place indoors of the twenty or so small boys ruled by Prout in his first essay in house-management.

By his friendliness and bonhomie Gigger was popular; and, having achieved popularity, he began to assert himself, in the usual way, by resenting the liberties taken by the cheeky ones, and putting them in their places, sometimes by verbal combat, sometimes on their backs on the floor. This interesting magnetic person, Gigs, seemed always crackling and sparkling and giving off electric shocks, often opening out vistas down which we saw extraordinary and little-understood things.

He instinctively avoided (though he was quite new at boarding-school life and its etiquettes and prohibitions) the mistakes that a tenderfoot generally makes. Thus he never incurred the ridicule and unpopularity that falls upon a newcomer who makes the mistake of parading his family advantages gratuitously and introducing the subject of his home privileges. He saw that the other small boys were very different from himself; and, although he had small experience of boys, he walked warily.

He certainly had the advantage of being placed among a lot of boys of whom none was much older than himself or more vigorous; so he was spared the annoyance or martyrdom of being an eccentric in a general company of larger boys some of whom might be empty-headed louts, who would amuse their vacuity by bullying any youngster who was available for these indulgences.

The headmaster, or the 'Head', always had an eye for Gigger – a rather indulgent one, though not going so far as favouritism. He was in a special sense *in loco parentis*, Gigger's parents, who were personal friends of the Head, being in India. In addition, Gigger was in his eyes a rather special jewel, as he was a junior member of a sacred band of artistic and literary lights who were teaching the London world, or part of it, all about art and literature.

This band was the Burne-Jones, Morris, Rossetti and Swinburne group, the so-called Pre-Raphaelites, and Gigger, being a nephew of Burne-Jones by marriage – in fact a nephew-in-law – was made of a different flesh and blood from the run and ruck of boys and belonged to an aristocracy of the mind, the mind creative; important, at least, in its own eyes and in the eyes of its disciples.

The Head was one of the very minor fiddles in the Pre-Raphaelite band as a result of the close friendship he had been fortunate enough to form with Burne-Jones at the Birmingham Grammar School, and with Morris at Oxford. These two celebrities had floated or steered themselves into the world's eye; and through them, in a sense, by diverse roads and winding ways the Head was to gain a sort of shadowy immortality as a faint ghost in fiction. . . .

Of course, the matter of chumming would depend on the tastes of the boys and the mutual similarity of outlooks and general agreement of ideas. Whether a boy preferred to talk about games or jackdaws or breaking bounds was a matter that decided friendship: a few like Gigger would talk about books, from the simple boys' stories to grown-ups' novels. One or two would discuss matters touched on in the dim mysterious regions of the mind where the more pretentious of the grown-ups disported themselves, or pretended they did.

Gigger's first signals for a craft of similar, or nearly similar, build were soon hung out. A mention of some author or some books not of the kind that catered for the tottering simplicities of tender youth was made and a response awaited. I remember the day, perhaps the second day after his arrival, when Gigger suddenly became aware that I shared his interest in this matter, or business, of letters and books. How his eyes brightened and his giglamps glittered! And thereupon, without many words, our alliance was struck up.

To me, Gigger was quite a find. What an extraordinary specimen to get into one's net! I had dragged through two other schools (preparatory ones); but here was a sample of something different in kind and not merely in degree. What a luxury to find one who had something to tell, who roamed in regions that were misty but interesting, and where there were exciting puzzles!

The few well-meaning boys that I had been mentor to could drop out and amuse and interest one another. This air was not for them to breathe. It was not nice to throw them off, but Gigger was too good to lose. Here was someone with something to give away instead of standing rather dumbly and slackly around and waiting to be entertained and amused. I felt properly fixed up with a chum like Gigger.

He was always interesting. Wherever one dug into him for information or to be diverted, there was something surely to reward the seeker – some strange way of looking at things, if nothing else. It was heartening, too, to see someone with a purpose other than that of merely dropping into a routine or profession, or the humdrum waiting for promotion that the army seemed to be: one who was going to adventure the slippery, treacherous roads of the arts. He couldn't, if the worse came to the worst, enlist as a Tommy; his short sight prevented that. As he said, it was sink or swim with him.

Between Gigger and me, literature was a constant bond. He would make inquiries as to what I had read and the kind of subjects I cared about. After asking about the more obvious writers, such as Scott and others of whom one could hardly avoid having heard, he would inquire whether I was acquainted with strange old folks of a long time back who wrote many things rather difficult to read and of whom I had never heard.

On learning my ignorance, he rather gathered himself up into a cloud of knowledge, very misty and obscure, where I could not follow him. He seemed to abide there a good deal and not to welcome visitors to it. He never troubled himself to set forth the matter or interest of whatever he was reading. Whether it was Chaucer, Froissart or Piers Plowman, or people who lived in Elizabeth's time, he never explained very much what their charm or attraction was. It was sufficient, perhaps, that they were rare and remote, not pawed over by the many.

Though his attitude towards the swarming mass of little boys seemed rather aloof, he was sometimes moved to take their mental state in hand. It really got on his nerves that they should keep on reading *Jack Harkaway* and the cheap paper-backed novels that were to be had in such plenty in those days, and which Gigger seemed to take as an infliction aimed especially at himself. The sight of a number of small boys, wet day after wet day – and there were plenty of wet days in Devonshire – sitting there reading what was to Gigger the veriest trash had a strange effect on his brain. It was like the dropping-water torture; it could not be endured indefinitely; and he inveighed against this type of literary pabulum, protesting that it led to softening of the brain.

But he met the fate of those idealists who do not quite understand the material with which they are dealing. Rage he never so wildly, the students of contemporary fiction continued their investigations with much the same assiduity as before the outburst.

It was a lesson to Gigger – his first contact, almost, with the obduracy of the human material with which a statesman has to work. He readjusted his conclusions, replaced his giglamps (after polishing the lenses), and came down many stages nearer to the level of the human boy.

It was not only out of school hours that the paperbacks were perused. A certain amount of learning had to be imbibèd at Westward Ho! in four or five daily doses of an hour each as we sat on the hard forms in class, and, to mitigate the frightful boredom of trying to absorb a lesson in French or geography or some other branch of polite learning, some boys used to continue their novel-reading while under the master's eye.

This surreptitious perusal of fiction often led to the confiscation of the work by the form-master, and thus to the loss of capital expenditure in addition to some other penalty. To obviate the total loss of an interesting little book, the Gigger set, active always against the aggressions of the enemy, formulated a system of tearing the few pages under perusal out of the main body of the book and bringing these only into class, leaving the bulk of the treasure in their lockers. This, of course, destroyed the book in the end, unless the pages so removed were carefully safeguarded. However, when the book was once read completely through, it was of no further interest, and its loss was of little account. . . .

Gigger did not come from a sporting family. It had never entered into his scheme of things to consider his neighbourhood solely from the point of view of how many sizable things there were to clear up and put an end to, and place on record in a game-book afterwards. His surroundings in the country were to him merely a place in which to dream or to think about the books he had read, and to observe the flux and flow of nature, and to consider the possibility of putting it all in a book. There was no special interest in the places where rabbits forgathered and perforated the crust of the earth, or where rats had their ill-omened abodes, or where the pesky, disgusting jackdaws, or whatever they were, fluttered annoyingly about.

Fell intent towards some breathing, moving being, against some order of evolution, should always be in the mind of the boy of action when sallying forth under the sky; but with Gigger one went out at peace with all the world of flying, scampering, wriggling things.

Fancy Gigger capering about after a butterfuly with a net! As well imagine old blind Milton gallivanting behind a flittering bat. He considered that his dignity as a man of letters precluded him from indulging in these childish pranks. Even the Natural History Society did not make him do more than raise his eyebrows, though he enrolled himself as a perfunctory member to please its founder, little Hartopp, who was so nice to him in Latin class.

There was only one biological thing I saw Gigger do, and that was really worth the while of a gigantic intellect. He produced on a plate in our big study a find worthy of Milton or Coleridge. It was nothing less than a frog which was being chawed to death, devoured alive, by hefty maggots, all inside him and coming out here and there through holes. Could Dante in lugubrious Ravenna or in the silence of the Pineta have joined himself to anything more stupendously tragic? This was the true zoological enterprise, the right thing for Gigger to deal with; in addition, it was a work of mercy of high ethical value. The skilful surgeon that he turned into was armed with a delicate pair of tweezers, and began with dexterous art to remove the maggots one by one, making them cease from their hideous task. He kept on dislodging them and placed them aside on another plate, presumably for some kind of execution.

This is so poignant a picture that memory refuses to register anything further than the spectacle of the amateur surgeon toiling philanthropically, or philfrogically, with his tweezers, and the patient, pitiful frog, the tearful *bonne-bouche*[1] of innumerable maggots: and also on the plate the pile of wriggling animalculae, destined to a crushing doom under a broad boot-sole. Then the whole scene fades.

And what of the frog? Here the most indefatigable and learned research can discover nothing, and one merely puts forward the surmise that the same boot-sole, the disease being incurable, made for this reptile a surcease to torture and to life. . . .

I have not entered very completely into the details of the interior decoration of our sanctum; but they should be touched on briefly now as leading to further developments.

Chiefly taking the eye, there was an ample bow-window, with a

glorious sea-view, at the end of the room. In this recess could be
arranged the stage for our great dramatic festivals; and to mark it off
from the body of the room we rigged up a splendid cretonne or
chintz curtain of startling pattern. The flouncing or looping up at
the sides of this noble decoration made a large demand on our
leisure time. It was worth it in our eyes. We belonged to the lineage
of those who would beggar themselves for magnificent surroundings
and largeness of living.

Before giving an account of the memorable performance of
Aladdin, or the Wonderful Scamp,[2] I may mentioned its precursor,
which was a powerful impersonation by Gigger of the principal
character in a drama called *Drink*.[3]

Drink, which was by Charles Reade, novelist and playwright, was
produced in the late seventies in London, with notable success. A
delirium tremens scene was one of the high spots of the action. This
scene took Gigger's fancy when he saw the play during one
Christmas holidays in London, and he was avid to pass on his
experience. So he gave us, in the big study, a version of the great
metropolitan hit.

Some good London actor had 'created' the principal part; and
our bard imitated this artist with excessive violence – most fantastic
wriggles and much over-acting. He would sit on a chair and
gradually work himself into convulsions, drawing down the corners
of his mouth and trying to make his eyes look terrible behind his
giglamps. By degrees he would slip off the chair to the floor and
grovel and work himself about like a very fat worm, growling and
moaning. Select audiences drawn from the intellectual *élite* of the
school would witness these paroxysms. At their conclusion, Gigger
would rise up, perspiring and panting, and bow in reply to the
applause. Then he would start gently deprecating his histrionic
abilities. He got rather angry if anybody took his self-depreciation
too seriously.

Gigger became a little uppish about all this and would have liked
to show off his convulsions in class instead of doing Latin Construes.
The rest of the study began to get jealous; and it came to be very
plainly seen that the only thing to do was to have a complete play,
giving everybody a part, so that all could share in the applause that
Gigger was having all to himself.

The next thing was to choose a play. The study had its own ideas
about the drama. They were not blown about by every gust of
passionate discussion, nor were they victims of every new school of

thought. They did not enter into long psychological discussions on the problem aspect of the question. In fact they held firmly to the sound Victorian principle that the best play was the play that had the largest number of puns.

So they sent to French's[4] for a couple of dozen choice samples of this type of drama, and, when they arrived, the whole five occupants of the study, neglecting all other work, sat down to count the puns. The job took a long time. Gigger was severely reprimanded because he had passed over two or three puns in going through a play. He had no excuse for being careless in a matter of art.

At last, *Aladdin or the Wonderful Scamp*, came out with top score – three puns above any other play. It was chosen, and everybody was provided with a book. As a prelude, Gigger kindly explained that the hero's name should be pronounced Allah-deen to be truly Persian; we adopted this pronunciation and felt some inches taller, looking down on the other boys who wallowed in a purely Britannic ignorance, innocent of the great Arabian tongue, unmindful of the storied East. We implied that Aladdin was a new play by a foreign dramatist (our own discovery); the others knew no better.

Then began the struggle for the parts. Each boy wanted the longest and most important part for himself. The matter was at last decided by the simple material arguments of pounds avoirdupois and the ability to use the fist. Thus Tuppenny became Aladdin; Potiphar, Abanazar; Tiddlewinks, the Princess Badroulbadour; Stalky (not a member of the study), the Sultan; and Gigger secured the part of Widow Twanky. To M'Turk was left the obscure character of the Executioner.

There was no stage-manager; such an individual would not have been tolerated for a moment. The parts were learned in school hours, of course. It was an expensive method of study in the matter of impositions, but the only honourable course to pursue. The study would have lost all self-respect if they had learned their parts in play-time. Owing to the absence of a stage-manager, there was a certain amount of confusion and difference of opinion in the rehearsals which led to unanticipated dramatic interludes. This only added force to the representation.

When the matter of costumes came up for discussion, M'Turk was astonished to find all the others unanimous on the question, and most curt. They were to make their own costumes. Why such unbridled ambition? Not a single one of them (above all, not

Gigger) was capable of handling a needle effectively. Still, the fiat went forth, though the study was in funds at the time. It was also passed, *nem. con.*,[5] that M'Turk should start first on his costume to show the others the way over. This he did. Being only allowed the very smallest capital from the common fund, he was obliged to use his cricket suit as a basis for his creation, and he proposed to decorate it lavishly with tinsel and coloured paper.

But Gigger persuaded them all that it would be far better for persons of cultivated taste to forsake 'the garish vulgarity of mere popular theatricalities', to eschew 'gaudy pretentiousness', and instead adopt a fine tone-effect by using brown paper only. This converted them all with amazing swiftness, and M'Turk was obliged to confine himself simply to brown paper. It struck him as queer, though, that none of the others was in any haste to follow his example and begin work on his own costume. They all said testily in reply to his inquiries that 'it would be all right on the night' and he was to leave it to them.

He left it to them till the very day of the performance. Then, stumbling into the study in the afternoon, he found them all trembling, excited and mad with delight over a large box of silk and velvet and cloth of gold. He could get no explanation at first. They merely flung the glittering raiment over themselves and danced about the room, screaming with glee. The label on the box showed that it was a case of theatrical costumes from Nathan. What, now, about 'gaudy pretentiousness' and 'garish vulgarity of popular theatricalities'?

They explained to M'Turk's chap-fallen face that the whole thing was accidental; they hadn't really known the day was so near. When the true state of affairs had dawned on them suddenly, the night before last, they had sent post-haste to Nathan because they really could not disappoint their guests; and they really found they had not after all M'Turk's great abilities in the tailoring line.

In the evening, everything was arranged with great care: the seats placed for the intellectuals of the school – about twenty-five all told – the final touches given to the stage. The dresses were put on and off frequently, and a looking-glass smuggled out of a dormitory, in which the players could admire themselves. It was rather a hot corner where the looking-glass was, and the dresses suffered. M'Turk kept out of it. It didn't seem worth bothering about a looking-glass for a little brown paper.

They all finally arranged themselves for the performance and paraded about – Gigger as Widow Twanky in an elaborate brocaded gown covered with gold lace, proud as Punch, with a huge chin projecting underneath a gray horsehair wig and a pair of spectacles. The performance began when all the audience had trooped in and taken their places. They were kept waiting a few minutes for the sake of impressiveness. Those few minutes were the only quiet time the study saw that night. Then the curtain rose.

Why enter into a detailed description or criticism of the piece? It was more like a football scrimmage than a properly organised theatrical representation. The puns were all screamed in chorus even by people off the stage. The performance nearly came to an end in a dispute between Gigger and Tuppenny over a pun, each claiming it for himself. They yelled and screamed it repeatedly, in each other's face with supreme contempt for the audience or the book. Then they fell to blows, there on the stage, and tore each other's dress. They had to be hauled off by people in the wings before the next scene could be proceeded with.

After the theatricals, there was, of course, a gorge, and everybody filled themselves with pilchards and washed the whole lot down with cocoa. Gigger, amongst others, was awakened in the night with violent pains and reconsidered his supper during the small hours, to the furious remonstrances of the dormitory.

When it came to sending back the apparel, it was a very sorry collection of torn and stained dresses, or rather parts of dresses, that was stuffed into the box. Nathan protested volubly on the arrival of the box in London, saying he did not know what it was that was in it and asking where the costumes were that he had sent. This led to a lengthy correspondence. Gigger was put on to it. He can be seen now in the mind's eye, curled up on a chair writing, his fat face wobbling over the brass-bound mahogany desk where he kept all his poems and other literary treasures.

He entered into prolonged discussions with Nathan – the study never let him off under an eight-page letter. He maintained that the costumes had arrived torn, that there were nails sticking up inside the box, and that the dresses must have been torn again in the same way on the return journey. Amongst other innumerable pleas was the suggestion that perhaps the porters had broken open the box and given a performance in the guard's van.

This brought the railway company into it. There was now a double correspondence going on. At the twelfth letter to the traffic-manager and the sixteenth to Nathan, Gigger sent each a poem. He had had this in reserve all along; it was his trump card. Nathan and the traffic-manager now chucked up the sponge and cut their losses . . .

The *Chronicle* – the *United Services College Chronicle*, each number now worth 12 guineas if the set is complete – was an epoch-making and formative influence for our Gigger. It had been in a state of suspended animation for some terms – or was it years? What a happiness it must have meant to Gigger when the Head first mooted its revival – with Gigger as editor. Editor! – making the thing almost what he liked! True, the Head said he himself would be editor, but that was only a matter of form; so that the Head could act as censor. It would be Gigger who would shape and order everything; the Head would have no time; he would let in the stuff that Gigger wanted in.

The old *Chronicle* – yes. Some giant figures in the misty past had been able so to wield their mighty pens that the product was actually worthy of print, worthy of being set up by comps in a Bideford printing-office. And the result was fairly grammatical, if not logical, and could appear before kindly critical eyes without arousing laughter or sneers or tears.

There were three back numbers in the Head's library, only three, and Gigger looked at them, holding them with trembling hands. Could he come up to their level, the height of the great prefects of old who had put forth their fancies in print? Well, after all, on careful examination, they were not so very grand, these little essays or screeds, and most of the paper was taken up with records of games and school doings – mechanical routine stuff. These youths had not been so very brainy; they seldom ventured into *belles-lettres*, little articles that would interest outsiders who were not all wrapped up in the doings and scramblings of school life.

Gigger was sure he could do the 'literary touch', the leader, commentary, sketch, editorial utterance, quite as well as those other fellows who were only material to fill up Woolwich or Sandhurst.

Why, verse! Of course! I was forgetting that for the moment. Verse! Those fellows couldn't do it at all, practically. One can shove verse in, if pat and not too stinging, and refer generally in rhyme to the Coll or Coll themes. What a vista! But no high-falutin', no would-be-fine writing, no sentimentalism – just surface stuff, witty, sparkling, laughter-raising, but not boisterously comic.

Yes, Gigger would take it on. How he thanked the Head, who guaranteed that the Coll would pay all expenses if the magazine didn't meet the costs! Gigger was good at thanking.

Gigger went out for a walk all by himself; he didn't want anybody with him. Visions and dreams flared sky high and branched out in all directions. What couldn't it lead to? Be sensible; it's only a little school magazine; still, under his own hand, pliant to his will and pleasure, with no stupid prefect over him to put a heavy foot on his wittiest stuff, his best verses, not seeing the point.

Gigger could make a little gem of it; each number a work of art, dainty as a flower. But no! There were all those horrid, stupid matches to go in, and scores, cricket scores. Perhaps the *Chronicle* wouldn't be a *Tatler* or *Rambler* or other classic. But you can't have everything handed to you absolutely perfect on a silver plate – and what a thing to happen anyway!

Gigger felt he had done nothing to earn it; it was only because the Head was a family friend. Still, who else was there in the Coll who had literary ambitions? And, above all, who was there, or who had there been, who could touch him in verse? With an easy mind Gigger could go his way; nobody would try to trip him up or be loud in sneers and hostile criticism, saying others could do much better and it was a scandal that Gigger was editor. There was only that other fellow, the second prefect, who thought himself a great literary gun; but he never put forth anything of his own, though always looking as if he was just going to. He wouldn't want to give hostages to detraction, or he might tumble off his high perch. The *Chronicle* was a rose without a thorn, or with only very little thorns.

And so Gigger, dreaming and scheming, rambled on, almost out of bounds, hardly knowing where he was going. He pulled up in time. It would never do to be hauled up as a little defaulting schoolboy when one had in spirit just about touched the summit of the calling of literature.

He went back to the study to talk to those two, Stalky and M'Turk; they would look much smaller now than they had done in the morning. Those two – yes, they might be a kind of staff if he wanted one..Leaning with both hands on the table, with glittering eyes and his smile, he announced to them that the Head had made him editor of the *Chronicle*, that was to be born again. They looked surprised; it was the first they had heard of it. They said how glad they were to hear he would be so well employed and not idle about pretending to work; but most likely he'd have to write all the paper

himself; they didn't know if, in this fine weather, anybody would
care to try to do anything for the magazine. Gigger said they two
would have to write something each – surely they could do it;
M'Turk read enough stuff to give some of it out again.

They promised in a high-hearted, optimistic way that they would
try, but searched vaguely round the inside of their heads, strangely
empty when it came actually to writing something and not merely
hoping and talking. Writing, they found, did not come of itself; and
strenuous effort seemed to drive away any half-caught ideas. At last
they had to give up without a word upon the paper, and go out to
punt about, to the beach, or to the tuck-shop. They might get ideas
in one of these places and come back refreshed and write about
various things at great length.

Gigger didn't want the masters to write anything; to make it a
masters' *Chronicle* would be feeble and silly. It was the boys' chance
to say something on their own account and kick free of the masters,
who had it all their own way in class-time. The two said they would
write about the masters, showing them up and their tricks and
dodges; or about the Coll, how badly things were managed; or
about the meals, how they should be much better.

Gigger said they knew that was all rot, and that the Head was
editor over him, or superior censor, and would have nothing of that
sort in the magazine. It took all the Head's time and cleverness to
expound to parents and people like that how splendid everything
was, and perfect; if he was faced with all their complaints in cold
print, he could never tell his fairy stories any more – he might even
cane somebody as a beginning if he read the MS.

The two said that if people were to be caned for writing articles
for the *Chronicle*, even if unaccepted, then Gigger had better do all
the writing himself. So this talk, instead of recruiting the staff,
reduced it again to one member. Never mind, the paper only
appeared at most once a month, and Gigger could do it all himself –
helped out by cricket scores and other stupid rot.

Yes! That was the idea! With no staff one would not quarrel with
other people over unsuitable articles or badly written ones. It was
lucky he had talked about caning; now things were much simpler;
he knew just what he had to do, and if prose gave out, or when he
could not think of anything fresh to write about, then he could jingle
on with verse. If that failed, there were parodies; he could just look
out something in the Browning book and go over it and turn it inside
out, when it would be as understandable as it was the other way

round. It would look wonderful to those other fellows who couldn't do it.

So the *Chronicle* was fairly started, and Gigger settled down to his first number in the Head's library, with the back numbers before him – three only – as examples of quantity and form, but not quality.

Well, good luck to you, Gigger! Do your little best now with your little independent command, your little company or squad of words and phrases, marching off on the long road to fame or forgetfulness.

Thus was the *Chronicle* started, or restarted. Nobody seemed to think he owed any duty to the little sheet, and once, when I was asked why I did not contribute something to it, I replied, 'Oh, it is such a small thing.' The riposte of the inquirer came quickly: 'Oh! you want to write for *The Times*, I suppose.'

Well, those *Chronicles* were not ludicrously smaller than *The Times* – as journals to write for. Their seven issues are remembered longer than seven contemporary issues of *The Times*. Nobody is giving £20 each for back numbers of *The Times* of the 'eighties.

Though one looked down from a great height on the diminutive news-sheet, one didn't deny the silver sixpence for its acquirement – that would have been too mean; a failure to support the panting, perspiring Gigger on his little enterprise. Give the bantling a chance to live, though there was 'nothing in the *Chronicle* again!'

Gigger was full of importance really, but not showing it – the editor of an influential paper, the biggest journalistic thing within a two-mile radius, the intellectual power-house of Bideford Bay. We told Gigger he could look out to the horizon, to the west, from Hartland Point to Baggy Point, and see nothing more brainy than he. Then some of us asked him if he had noticed the donkeys that were hired out for rides on the sands; and begged him to consider where he would place them in the intellectual scale with relation to himself.

Gradually it was borne upon us that Gigger could write so as to be acceptable to a prospective audience, even a schoolboy one. Yet it is pathetic to think that all his skill and art gained so little recognition or compliment from the Devonshire mob standing round. Perhaps we largely missed his points. I know I didn't congratulate him; we took it as a matter of course that Gigger should turn out his stuff and that we could not; but we didn't rate ourselves any lower on that account. We were as good as he was, but we kept it all inside; that was the unction we laid to our souls.

Even the masters took a depreciatory view of Gigger, who was no scholar as they were in Latin or Greek. 'It's no use making out he's anything wonderful because he writes that wretched *Chronicle* – nearly all. When he gets out into the scramble of things he won't find it so easy; other stronger writers will push him into a corner. Those that count won't be a cap in hand to him, like people are here, letting him do everything' – such might be the misty musings of the average master.

Gigger had to fight through a thicket of rather dark trouble before he he could express himself in masterly prose; he had to force his way through verse. The ideas that would bob up in his head all clothed in their rub-a-dub dress had to be persuaded to put on a more simple costume. It took time. One or two of us thought he would never do it, and laughed to see him floundering about, sloughing off the Johnsonese and journalese, puffing and blowing and wriggling and perspiring in his chair, his nose on his paper, of course. He would get frightfully angry; he couldn't keep his feet still while he was at it. We knew when he was writing prose by the sighs that went off and by the paper – the foolscap. When Gigger did verse, it was done with great respect to the Muse on our best cream-laid notepaper.

He kept asking for contributions, suggesting that we, or I, should do something. But he didn't beg or pray or urge; if you wouldn't – or couldn't, more like – he just did a bit more himself – a camel-like fellow; you could keep putting on loads and more loads, he didn't complain.

Gigger maintained that all sorts of articles in the *Chronicle* suggested themselves, and could be written, or at least started. A friend of Stalky's suggested that the masters might be 'done' by pretending that caricatures of them were really about masters at other schools one had been at; but Gigger put a stopper to that.

Then what about the Pebble Ridge.[6] Fellows could have scribbled a lot about that – how long it was, how high, how wide; then multiply something by something and it would all be as clear as mud. Suppose it was all piled up in a pyramid in Hyde Park; would it push the railings over? What was the weight of it? What force per something did the sea need, to push it back some feet every year? And if that force was exerted the other way on, and the Pebble Ridge went out to sea, by how much would England be bigger annually?

But Gigger couldn't stand anything about something per

something, with figures at each end and signs and things in the middle; he hated numbers and figures; and yet Pope says of another wretched Gigger he 'lisped in numbers for the numbers came'. We threw that at Gigger every now and then to calm him down and show him there were plenty more like him or better; and, what's more, there always had been; he was no new wonder, and never would be. If we two, Stalky and I, had rhyming dictionaries, we could do as well as he did with verses and poems. You only had to put the rhymes at the end of the lines and fill in the beginnings and middles with words – words! And the dictionary was full of them, to use as you liked.

Gigger didn't actually need a rhyming dictionary because he had rhymes in his head – which must be a pesky nuisance, I thought. I pitied poor Gigger. He couldn't help scribbling, so long as it had nothing to do with school-work. He kept spoiling reams – absolute reams, not quires – of cream-laid notepaper for poems; they must have been poems, because the lines were shortish and ended raggedly; his Latin books were on the floor and his foot on an open dictionary. When you told him about the dictionary and that the blacking was all over the print, he cursed you and gave the book a good hefty kick to the other side of the room.

We felt it a rotten thing to be messed and muddled up with poems that Gigger showed to nobody and objected to anybody's looking at. He said they were letters to his mater; not even a cad would look at letters to a mater. Besides, he was asking for money, and you oughtn't to humbug that up.

If he could only shut up this paper-spoiling and get the whole thing out of his head, he might be top of King's[7] Latin class, we think. He's as sharp as a weasel about other things. But, as it is, the podgy Giglamps can't even form good resolutions; doesn't try to; says, 'Damn the preparation' without a thought as to what he is doing with his time.

King said he'd 'die in a garret a scurrilous pamphleteer'. I heard him say it; but I wondered what that really was. I suppose King was serious about it. Well, well, Gigger was somebody to swear at, and tell how wrong he was going; somebody to point at and say he was going to make a bigger mess of things in his life than you were.

NOTES·

Of Irish descent, George Charles Beresford (1865–1938) – despite a sharp tongue and, in later years, a growing sense of disappointment in the development of his own career – took justifiable pride in the closeness of his friendship to Kipling. As an admirer of Ruskin and Carlyle at Westward Ho!, he stimulated Kipling's readings in the works of these difficult authors. He later became a civil engineer in India, and joined the Fabian Society. He is the real M'Turk of *Stalky & Co.*, and one of the founders of the Kipling Society. He exhibited at the Royal Academy, and achieved distinction as both a photographer and an antique-dealer.

1. A good or pleasant taste in one's mouth.

2. A student reworking of *Aladdin and the Wonderful Lamp*, by John Maddison Morton (1856).

3. Charles Reade's most effective play (1879), adapted from the plot of Zola's *L'Assommoir*.

4. Publisher of acting editions of plays.

5. *Nemine contradicente* (no one contradicting).

6. 'When you looked at it for the first time, the Ridge seemed like the giraffe at the Zoo; you felt inclined not to believe it. It was just a bank of large boulders each about the size of a football. It was perhaps 15 feet high and 50 yards broad, and seemed of human construction; as if some industrious navvies had placed it there but forgotten the cement. The summit was a sharp ridge: the whole, the work of old Ocean and placed at the highest limit of the tides' – Beresford, *School-days with Kipling*, p. 49.

7. Kipling's portrait of 'King' in *Stalky and Co.* seems to be based not only upon William Crofts, the schoolmaster who taught Kipling both Latin and English, but also upon another Latin teacher, F. W. Haslam.

Westward Ho! Reminiscences

J. C. RIMINGTON

Now comes the difficult task of describing Kipling, the schoolboy – difficult because my recollection of him is chiefly in his capacity as editor of the school *Chronicle*. He was not outstandingly popular: not that he was unpopular, for he was always bright and cheerful and had a ready tongue, but his weak eyesight prevented him from playing games, and that is always a handicap amongst boys. Strange to say, he did not shine much in Latin; French he knew well, and of course he had a brilliant knowledge of English literature. His literary skill was early recognised as he was made editor and principal contributor to the *Chronicle*, and excellent stuff he put into it. Unfortunately, I did not keep my copies of the

* *Kipling Journal*, VIII (July 1941) 6–7.

Chronicle; had I done so, they would now have been worth their weight in gold; but there is one verse from it which, on account of its 'jingle', or from the fact that it was about 'tuck', has stayed in my memory all these many years. In one of the studies, the boys, while cooking, had set fire to the curtains, and unwittingly had done their best to burn the College down. This evoked an edict from authority that, except in prefects' studies, all cooking was forbidden. This prohibition of 'brewing' gave Kipling a chance to respond with this burning effusion:

> The cup is devoid of its coffee
> The spoon of its sugary load
> The tablecloth guiltless of toffee
> And sorrow has seized our abode.
> We once that were bloated with brewing
> We once that were broad of the beam
> Are wasted and wan from eschewing
> All dainties of bun, jam and cream.

(There is, I am told, a slight inaccuracy in some of the wording, but that is how it has stuck in my memory, and I have had neither the opportunity nor the desire to alter it.)

That noble confection 'bun, jam and cream' deserves a worthy description: it consisted of a beautiful big bun, much larger than the ordinary bun of today, cut in half horizontally with a solid slab of jam on the lower half, covered with a generous measure of rich Devonshire cream and the top half replaced as a cap for the whole: it was thus about two inches thick. The cost of this delicacy was $1\frac{1}{2}$ d. It had one great merit that after one had consumed the bun, there was the further ecstasy of licking off the jam and cream which had exuded onto one's cheeks! Sergeant Kyte, who ran the tuck shop, was a great, gaunt, kindly, ex-cavalry man, who was reported, I believe with truth, to have taken part in the Charge of the Light Brigade at Balaclava. He may have been once a fierce trooper but he had a generous and soft heart for boys.

NOTE

General Joseph Cameron Rimington (1864–1942) entered the Royal Engineers in 1884; served in Burma (1886–7), the First World War (as Engineer-in-Chief in Mesopotamia, 1915–19), and India (General Military Works, Army Headquarters, 1919–21).

Part III
Journalism in India

My First Book*

RUDYARD KIPLING

As there is only one man in charge of a steamer, so there is but one man in charge of a newspaper, and he is the editor. My chief[1] taught me this on an Indian journal, and he further explained that an order was an order, to be obeyed at a run, not a walk, and that any notion or notions as to the fitness or unfitness of any particular kind of work for the young had better be held over till the last page was locked up to press. He was breaking me into harness, and I owe him a deep debt of gratitude, which I did not discharge at the time. The path of virtue was very steep, whereas the writing of verses allowed a certain play to the mind, and, unlike the filling-in of reading-matter, could be done as the spirit served. Now a sub-editor is not hired to write verses. He is paid to sub-edit. At the time, this discovery shocked me greatly; but, some years later, when, for a few weeks I came to be an editor-in-charge, Providence dealt me for my subordinate one saturated with Elia. He wrote very pretty, Lamb-like essays, but he wrote them when he should have been sub-editing. Then I saw a little what my chief must have suffered on my account. There is a moral here for the ambitious and aspiring who are oppressed by their superiors.

This is a digression, as all my verses were digressions from office work. They came without invitation, unmanneredly, in the nature of things; but they had to come, and the writing out of them kept me healthy and amused. To the best of my remembrance, no one then discovered their grievous cynicism, or their pessimistic tendency, and was far too busy, and too happy, to take thought about these things.

So they arrived merrily, being born out of the life about me, and they were very bad indeed; but the joy of doing them was pay a

* *Works*, Burwash Edition (New York: Doubleday, Doran, 1941; repr. New York: AMS Press, 1970) vol. XXIII, pp. 353-7.

thousand times their worth. Some, of course, came and ran away
again and the dear sorrow of going in search of these (out of office
hours) and catching them, was almost better than writing them
clear. Bad as they were, I burned twice as many as were published,
and of the survivors at least two-thirds were cut down at the last
moment. Nothing can be wholly beautiful that is not useful, and
therefore my verses were made to ease off the perpetual strife
between the manager extending his advertisements, and my chief
fighting for his reading-matter. They were born to be sacrificed.
Rukn-Din, the foreman of our side, approved of them
immensely, for he was a Muslim of culture. He would say, 'Your
poetry very good, sir; just coming proper length today. You giving
more soon? One-third column just proper. Always can take on third
page.'

Mahmoud, who set them up, had an unpleasant way of referring
to a new lyric as '*Ek aur chiz*' – 'one more thing' – which I never liked.
The job side, too, were unsympathetic, because I used to raid into
their type for private proofs with Old English and Gothic headlines.
Even a Hindu does not like to find the serifs of his 'f's cut away to
make long 's's.

And in this manner, week by week, my verses came to be printed
in the paper. I was in very good company, for there is always an
undercurrent of song, a little bitter for the most part, running
through the Indian papers. The bulk of it is much better than mine,
being more graceful, and is done by those less than Sir Alfred
Lyall[2] – to whom I would apologise for mentioning his name in this
gallery – 'Pekin', 'Latakia', 'Cigarette', 'O', 'TW', 'Foresight', and
others, whose names came up with the stars out of the Indian Ocean
going eastward.

Sometimes a man in Bangalore[3] would be moved to song, and a
man on the Bombay side would answer him, and a man in Bengal
would echo back, till at last we would all be crowing together, like
cocks before daybreak, when it is too dark to see your fellow. And,
occasionally, some unhappy Chaaszee, away in the China Ports,
would lift up his voice among the tea-chests, and the queer-smelling
yellow papers of the Far East brought us his sorrows. The
newspaper files showed that, forty years ago, the men sang of just the
same subjects as we did – of heat, loneliness, love, lack of promotion,
poverty, sport, and war. Further back still, at the end of the
eighteenth century, Hickey's *Bengal Gazette*,[4] a very wicked little
sheet in Calcutta, published the songs of the young factors, ensigns,

and writers to the East India Company. They, too, wrote of the same things, but in those days men were strong enough to buy a bullock's heart for dinner, cook it with their own hands, because they could not afford a servant, and make a rhymed jest of all the squalor and poverty. Lives were not worth two monsoons' purchase, and perhaps a knowledge of this a little coloured the rhymes when they sang:

> In a very short time you're released from all cares –
> If the Padre's asleep, Mr Oldham reads prayers!

The note of physical discomfort that runs through so much Anglo-Indian poetry had been struck then. You will find it most fully suggested in 'The Long, Long Indian Day', a comparatively modern affair; but there is a set of verses called 'Scanty Ninety-five', dated about Warren Hastings's time, which gives a lively idea of what our seniors in the service had to put up with. One of the most interesting poems I ever found was written at Meerut,[5] three or four days before the Mutiny broke out there. The author complained that he could not get his clothes washed nicely that week, and was very facetious over his worries!

My verses had the good fortune to last a little longer than some others, which were more true to facts, and certainly better workmanship. Men in the Army and the Civil Service and the Railway wrote to me saying that the rhymes might be made into a book. Some of them had been sung to the banjoes round the camp-fires, and some had run as far down coast as Rangoon[6] and Moulmein,[7] and up to Mandalay.[8] A real book was out of the question, but I knew that Rukn-Din and the office plant were at my disposal at a price, if I did not use the office time. Also, I had handled in the previous year a couple of small books, of which I was part owner, and had lost nothing. So there was built a sort of book, a lean oblong docket, wire-stitched, to imitate a DO[9] Government envelope, printed on one side only, bound in brown paper, and secured with red tape. It was addressed to all heads of departments, and all Government officials, and among a pile of papers would have deceived a clerk of twenty years' service. Of these 'books' we made some hundreds, and as there was no necessity for advertising, my public being to my hand, I took reply-postcards, printed the news of the birth of the book on one side, the blank order-form on the other, and posted them up and down the Empire from Aden to

Singapore and from Quetta[10] to Colombo.[11] There was no trade discount, no reckoning twelves as thirteens, no commission, and no credit of any kind whatever. The money came back in poor but honest rupees, and was transferred from the publisher, my left-hand pocket, direct to the author, my right-hand pocket. Every copy sold in a few weeks, and the ratio of expenses to profits, as I remember it, has since prevented my injuring my health by sympathising with publishers who talk of their risks and advertisements. The down-country papers complained of the form of the thing. The wire-binding cut the pages, and the red tape tore the covers. This was not intentional, but Heaven helps those who help themselves. Consequently, there arose a demand for a new edition, and this time I exchanged the pleasure of taking in money over the counter for that of seeing a real publisher's imprint on the title page. More verses were taken out and put in, and some of that edition travelled as far as Hong Kong on the map, and each edition grew a little fatter and, at last, the book came to London with a gilt top and a stiff back, and was advertised in a publisher's poetry department.

But I loved it best when it was a little brown baby, with a pink string round its stomach; a child's child, ignorant that it was afflicted with all the most modern ailments; and before people had learned beyond doubt how its author lay awake of nights in India, plotting and scheming to write something that should take with the English public.

NOTES

1. Kipling worked for Stephen Wheeler from 1883 to 1887, as assistant editor of the *Civil and Military Gazette*. Wheeler, who was somewhat conservative, may have resented Kipling's appearance as sub-editor, a position he had obtained through influence. Determined to reduce the number and fervency of Kipling's literary flourishes, Wheeler acted as a stern taskmaster for four years, forcing Kipling to perform prosaic duties (such as translating newspaper items from French-language Russian newspapers). In later years Kipling said that he appreciated the thoroughness of his apprenticeship. Kay Robinson replaced Wheeler, who by the summer of 1886 had become exhausted with fever. Wheeler returned to London, worked on the *St James's Gazette*, and performed one last important service for Kipling by introducing him to Sidney Low, the *Gazette's* editor, shortly after Kipling reached London.

2. Sir Alfred Comyn Lyall (1835–1911) was an Anglo-Indian civil administrator and man of letters. His writings include *Verses Written in India* (1889), *The Rise and Expansion of the British Dominion in India* (1929) and *Asiatic Studies* (1882).

3. Capital of the state of Mysore, India; now called Karnataka.

4. James Augustus Hickey established *Hickey's Bengal Gazette* in 1780. Articles

hostile to Warren Hastings resulted in Hickey's arrest, and the closing of the paper in 1782.

5. Trade centre and administrative headquarters of the Meerut district and division, Uttar Pradesh state, northern India, north-east of Delhi.

6. Capital of Burma.

7. Chief town of British Burma between 1826 and 1852; today the administrative headquarters of the Amherst district and of Tenasserim Division, Lower Burma.

8. The second biggest city of Burma; the last capital of the formerly independent kingdom of Upper Burma.

9. District office.

10. The capital of British Baluchistan, India, came under British rule in 1877. Its military significance derives from its commanding position over the main route, via the Balan Pass, between the lower Indus Valley and the Kandahar region of Afghanistan. Today Quetta is the chief town of the Baluchistan region of Pakistan. See Kipling's 'The Story of Uriah' in *Departmental Ditties and Other Verses* (1886).

11. Capital and chief port of Ceylon (modern Sri Lanka).

Rudyard Kipling's Early Association with Journalism*

CLIVE RATTIGAN

Accident plays a part in the lives of all men, be they small or great; and it was accident rather than any natural bent for the profession that made Rudyard Kipling start his career as a journalist. He was only seventeen at the time and though he was brimful of confidence in his own powers, with a ready wit in conversation and with a certain aptitude for story-telling, there was nothing to indicate that he was possessed of exceptional literary gifts. He owed his introduction to journalism indeed, to the simple facts that a career of some sort had to be found for him and that his parents, Mr and Mrs Lockwood Kipling, were extremely popular members of Lahore society and were able without much difficulty to persuade the then onwners of the two Indian papers, the *Civil and Military Gazette* of Lahore and *The Pioneer* for Allahabad – the writer's own father, Sir

* *Kipling Journal*, no. 1 (Mar 1927) 31–2.

George Allen, and Sir James Walker[1]– to find him a billet as 'assistant editor'.

It was on the *Civil and Military Gazette* that Rudyard Kipling began his journalistic career and here again happy chance was the chief instrument in developing one side at least of his genius. One of the features of the Lahore paper in those days was the 'turnover' or short story occupying the last column of the front page and turning over on to the second page. Kipling soon made this 'turnover' his own special preserve. From being merely one of the features of the paper this short story rapidly became the feature that attracted most interest in each day's issue and the initials 'RK' exercised a magic charm over the wide territory in north-western and northern India whence the *Civil and Military Gazette* claimed and still claims its reading public.

Before Kipling migrated to Allahabad to join the staff of *The Pioneer* he had given evidence of extraordinary felicity in the writing of occasional verse; but neither at Lahore nor at Allahabad did he display any taste for the ordinary duties of an assistant editor. The composing of leaders or leaderettes was the task he preferred to leave to others; he would reel off with ease stories and little gems of verse whenever the mood seized him, but to write on any serious subject, in the grand editorial manner, was something quite beyond him. And so it came about that, when he was for leaving *The Pioneer*, the then manager solemnly assured him in all good faith that he would never do any good with his pen and had better take to some easier means of earning his livelihood.

Kipling had departed from *The Pioneer* many years before I joined it, but his association with it was something more than a mere memory as three at least of his former colleagues were still with the paper and could speak with personal knowledge of him and his methods of work. I remember being shown with much ceremony the very chair upon which Rudyard Kipling was wont to sit when littering his room with reams of rejected manuscript; I was regaled with countless tales as to how he would avoid the delights of Club society for a quiet chat with the inhabitants of some out-of-the-way corner in the city bazaar, and how he would forget to do the work that had been assigned to him and make good the omission by some priceless unasked-for contribution; and every now and then when I would be going through the old files of the paper I would come across some poem or story that had apparently escaped republication.

NOTES

Clive Rattigan was a member of a distinguished family. His father, William Rattigan, was one of the founders of the *Civil and Military Gazette*, along with James Walker (Kipling's first patron). William Rattigan and Walker purchased a controlling interest in *The Pioneer* after they had put the *Gazette* on a firm financial footing. As Angus Wilson has noted, William Rattigan's career in some respects resembles that of Kimball O'Hara in *Kim*. The son of an illiterate Irish private in the Indian Army, Sir William (1842–1904) rose to a judgeship in the Punjab Chief Court, vice-chancellorship of the Punjab University, and membership of the Governor General's legislative Council. Clive Rattigan edited both *The Pioneer* and the *Civil and Military Gazette*. Sir Terence Rattigan (coming down to modern times) has won distinction in the theatre.

1. The wealth of Sir James Walker came in large measure from the organisation of a transportation system between Simla and the Plains. As a friend of Lockwood and Alice Kipling, he found jobs for Rudyard. He also provided lodging for his employee whenever Rudyard visited Simla.

Kipling as a Journalist*

CLIVE RATTIGAN

It was my father, the late Sir William Rattigan, KC, MP, who gave Rudyard Kipling his first start in a literary career.

That was in 1882 when Kipling was only seventeen, a mere schoolboy who had only just left Westward Ho! At that time my father was practising at the Bar at Lahore and was the principal proprietor of two Indian newspapers, the *Civil and Military Gazette* at Lahore and *The Pioneer* at Allahabad.

He was a great friend of Rudyard's father, John Lockwood Kipling, Principal of the Art School of Lahore, and the Lockwood Kiplings, anxious to have their son with them in India, approached my father with the request that he should give Rudyard a job on the *Civil and Military Gazette*.

They frankly admitted that Rudyard had no journalistic qualifications – he was far too young to have had any experience of newspaper work; but he had, they said, a certain urge to write and a

* *Saturday Review*, CLXI (25 Jan 1936) 106–7.

gift for vigorous expression. They were confident he would prove in time a very competent journalist.

Realising the possibility that Rudyard might well have inherited the literary and artistic abilities of his parents, my father was quite prepared to make the experiment of adding an inexperienced youth to the staff of the Lahore paper. Accordingly, he consulted his fellow proprietors, and Rudyard was brought out to Lahore as an assistant editor.

In those days Indian newspaper staffs were extremely small and every member, not excluding the editor, had to perform multifarious duties such as 'sub-ing', reporting and extensive proof-reading.

News from abroad came almost entirely by mail, and inland telegraphic news was meagre in the extreme. With poor railway services and other means of transport over vast tracts of country confined to horse-driven vehicles, there was little hope of news-papers attaining large circulations, even if the English-reading public had been, what it was not, extensive.

The lack of transport facilities and the limitations to circulation resulted in the absence of that flurry and bustle associated with modern newspaper life.

And, with more time at their disposal and little need to concern themselves with the up-to-dateness of their general news, Indian journalists in the 'eighties took particular pains to make their newspapers interesting to the public they served.

That public, if small, was a very intelligent one, thoroughly appreciative of literary grace and piquancy in short story, special article or editorial comment.

And, as is inevitable with a comparatively small society, every man's or woman's life was apt to be a open book to his or her neighbours. This afforded plenty of scope for the personal note in newspaper criticism or story.

Indian politics at that time did not trouble the journalist. The Indian National Congress[1] was not founded till three years after Rudyard reached Lahore, and at the beginning it was a very mild affair, among its 'fundamental principles', as laid down by its founder, the ex-Indian civilian, Allan Octavian Hume,[2] being 'the consolidation of union between England and India'.

Rudyard attended one of its earlier meetings on behalf of *The Pioneer* and his rather slighting comments on one of the speakers proved rather expensive, since it caused a libel action to be brought against the Allahabad paper. But that, as he would have said, is another story.

For the most part English-edited papers in India had little concern with Indian nation-building or Indian political demands. There were no Indian members of Council, no Indian governors, no Indian secretaries to Government. The whole Indian official hierarchy was British.

The only effective criticism of that hierarchy was British, too. *The Pioneer* and the *Civil and Military Gazette*, while priding themselves on being semi-official organs of Government, did not hesitate on occasions to belabour the provincial authorities or the Government of India for what they conceived to be wrong-headed policy.

Such was the journalistic atmosphere into which this youth of seventeen was brought – an atmosphere in which he at once felt himself quite at home in view of his family's long residence in the country and its familiarity with the special conditions of Indian official life.

Rudyard quickly showed that he had no liking for purely routine work. His proofs would lie on his desk uncorrected to the disorganisation of the press, and assignments such as reports of local happenings would too often be completely forgotten. His editor would rave and storm, and Rudyard would be apologetic and promise to reform. But the same thing would happen over and over again.

Rudyard wanted to write, wanted to go out to Mian Mir,[3] where the troops were, and chat with Thomas Atkins[4] or saunter into the city and converse with anyone he could get into conversation with, or he had an idea for a story or verses ringing in his head. How could he be bothered with proofs or idiotic reports of gymkhanas,[5] Government House parties or polo matches?

One little corner of the *Civil and Military Gazette* specially appealed to him. This was the 'turnover' from the last column of the front page to the next page. It was the particular niche for the short story or sketch bearing the mystic initials 'RK' at the end. This 'turnover' in Rudyard's hands became a very distinctive feature of the paper and *Gazette* readers always looked for those initials and were sorely disappointed when they were absent.

As his short stories, sketches and 'Departmental Ditties' began to appear and Anglo-Indian society was observed to be chortling over the relentless exposure of its weaknesses and failings, Rudyard's colleagues at Lahore learnt to make allowances for his journalistic eccentricities and to relieve him of duties that interfered with his writing or his collection of 'copy'.

His reputation, of course, had preceded him when he was transferred to Allahabad, but there he found he could not be let off journalistic duties so lightly, since there was more work to be done in the way of descriptive and other reporting, in sub-editing and in correcting proofs, *The Pioneer* having then become the leading paper of India.

Rudyard, as at Lahore, could not adapt himself to journalistic routine. He still neglected his proofs, still left urgent copy unsub-edited on his desk, still forgot the engagements for which he had been booked.

He made up for these deficiencies by sparkling verse or masterly short story.

His editor appreciated his genius, but it is to be feared the management did not.

It may have been the press delays resulting from Rudyard's forgetfulness that rankled or it may have been perhaps the expense of that libel case. At any rate the Allahabad manager did not heave any sigh of regret when Rudyard announced that he was giving up journalism and going home to England after a tour of the Far East.

The manager wished him every good wish, but delivered his Parthian shot: 'I am afraid, my dear fellow, you'll never make your fortune with your pen.'

NOTES

1. Founded in 1885.

2. Hume (1829–1912) served in the Departments of Customs, Agriculture and Judiciary. A member of the Indian Civil Service, he took a major role in organising and supporting the National Congress. He wrote several works on ornithology.

3. Kipling's interest was in the cantonment. But that, in turn, derived its name from Mohammed Mir, a saint revered in the region.

4. Kipling used the name when talking about the British private soldier, but the casual use of the name on the specimen forms of the official regulations was a practice dating back to at least 1815.

5. Places such as clubs in which materials needed for athletics and games are provided.

Kipling in India*

E. KAY ROBINSON

Although my official relations with Kipling did not commence till the autumn of 1886, our acquaintance on paper opened almost immediately after my arrival in India in January 1885. I had written some dog-Latin verses in *The Pioneer* of Allahabad, to which paper I had gone out as assistant editor, and signed them with my initials 'KR', being unaware that Kipling, who was assistant editor of the *Civil and Military Gazette* of Lahore, was in the habit of sending verses to *The Pioneer*, signed 'RK'. I was unaware, indeed, of Kipling's existence, until I received a courteous letter from him, saying that he had been undeservedly complimented (!) upon the Latin verses, which owing to the similarity of our initials, were being attributed to him. I looked up the files of the paper for some of his work, and after reading it appreciated the honour done to my verses in the mistake.

The next incident which brought us into correspondence might also have annoyed a writer without Kipling's modesty and good temper. He had been commissioned to write a Christmas poem for *The Pioneer*, and he sent a copy of verses. They were harmonious, but instead of reflecting the traditional spirit of Yuletide, they satirised the incongruity of Christmas festivity in India, in the midst of an alien, heathen, and poverty-stricken people. The poem was altogether so 'unchristmassy' that it would have been rejected had it not passed through my hands in the *Pioneer* office. I wrote a parody of it, verse by verse, taking the same dolorous view of Christmas in London as Kipling had taken of Christmas in India; and, whereas he had suggested that only our brethren in England, with their holly and mistletoe, could really enjoy Christmas, I implied that India, with its blue skies and bright sunshine, was the place where the festive season might actually be worth enjoying. The two poems

* *McClure's Magazine*, VII (July 1896) 99–109.

were published side by side as 'Dyspeptic Views of Christmas', signed respectively 'RK' and 'KR'. Instead of being irritated by this perversion of the sentiment he had intended seriously, Kipling wrote me a letter of thanks.

Shortly afterwards I obtained a month's leave, and visited, among other places, Lahore, where I made the acquaintance of the Kipling family. A more charming circle it would be hard to find. John Lockwood Kipling, the father, a rare, genial soul, with happy artistic instincts, a polished literary style, and a generous, cynical sense of humour, was, without exception, the most delightful companion I had ever met. Mrs Kipling, the mother, preserved all the graces of youth, and had a sprightly, if occasionally caustic wit, which made her society always desirable. Miss Kipling, the sister, now Mrs Fleming, inherits all her mother's vivacity and possesses a rare literary memory. I believe that there is not a single line in any play of Shakespeare's which she cannot quote. She has a statuesque beauty, and in repose her face is marvellously like that of Mary Anderson.[1] With Kipling himself, I was disappointed at first. At the time of which I am writing, early in 1886, his face had not acquired the character of manhood, and contrasted somewhat unpleasantly with his stoop (acquired through much bending over an office table), his heavy eyebrows, his spectacles, and his sallow Anglo-Indian complexion; while his jerky speech and abrupt movements added to the unfavourable impression. But his conversation was brilliant, and his sterling character gleamed through the humorous light which shone behind his spectacles, and in ten minutes he fell into his natural place as the most striking member of a remarkably clever and charming family. It was a domestic quartette. They had combined, by the way, in the previous year, to produce 'The Quartette',[2] a Christmas publication of unusual ability; and each of the four had individually attained to almost as much literary fame as can be won in India.

It was inevitable that such a family, placed in such surroundings, should yield an atmosphere of domestic approval warm enough to be liable to encourage eccentric growth in Kipling's budding genius. He was compelled, however, to work daily in a newspaper office, under a man who appreciated his talent very little, and kept him employed on work for the most part utterly uncongenial; and this may have acted as a salutary antidote. Nevertheless, it is almost pathetic to look through the *Civil and Military Gazette* of that time and note where Kipling's bright humour only flashed out in the introductory lines to summaries of government reports, dry semi-political notes, and the side-headings of scissors-and-paste paragraphs. This, however, was the maximum of literary display usually allowed to him; and it seemed such waste of genius that I strongly urged him to go to England, where he would win real fame, and possibly wealth, instead of the few hundred depreciated rupees per month which are the guerdon of Anglo-Indian journalism. To all such suggestions he always returned the answer that when he *knew* he could do good work, it would be time for him to strive for a place in the English world of letters, and that, in any case, the proprietors of the *Civil and Military Gazette* had taken him on trust, a boy fresh from School, and he would serve them loyally, like Jacob in the Bible, for his full seven years. Whether he gained or lost thereby in the long run I do not know; but that I personally gained is certain, for to Kipling's refusal to leave India was due the fact that when I subsequently arrived at Lahore to take over the editorship of the *Civil and Military Gazette* I found him still there as assistant.

I also found a letter awaiting me from the chief proprietor, in which he expressed the hope that I would be able to 'put some sparkle into the paper'. When the staff of a journal consists of two men only, one of whom is Kipling, such an exhortation addressed to the other doubtless seems curious. But, as I have said above, Kipling had been discouraged from 'sparkling'. My predecessor in the editorship of the *Civil and Military Gazette* had done his best to make a sound second-rate journalist out of the youngster by keeping his nose at the grindstone of proof-reading, scissors-and-paste work, and the boiling down of government Blue Books into summaries for publication. But Kipling had the buoyancy of a cork, and, after his long office work, had still found spare energy to write those charming sketches and poems which in *Soldiers Three* and the *Departmental Ditties* gave him such fame as can be won in the narrow world of Anglo-India. The privilege which he most valued at this time was the permission to send such things as his editor refused for the *Civil and Military Gazette* to other papers for publication. These papers used to publish and pay for them gladly, and the compliments and encouragement with which more sympathetic critics treated his work, partly consoled him for the efforts made in his own office to curtail his exuberant literature.

Whatever may have been the reason for the repression to which Kipling had been subjected before my arrival at Lahore, the fact explains why I, instead of he, should have been asked to put some 'sparkle' into the paper. I read the letter to him, and we agreed that champagne had more of the desired quality than anything else we could think of; and as the 'Sind³ and Punjab Hotel' happened to be opposite our office, I sent over for a bottle, and we inaugurated our first day's work together by drinking to the successful sparkle of 'The Rag' under its new management. Among many cherished scraps of paper lost in a despatch box which was stolen from me in Italy, that land of thieves, on my way back from India, was a drawing in red ink, perpetrated partly by Kipling and partly by myself, of this initiatory symposium. I knew that Kipling was predestined to fame, and I kept this sketch as the first result of our collaboration. It represented our two selves seated at the office table, with champagne bottle and glasses, and was headed 'Puting Some Sparkle into It'. There were several fox-terriers (of sorts) in the picture – Kipling's 'Vic', 'Joe', my property, and 'Buz', a delightful performing terrier, belonging to somebody else, that had attached itself to us and our dogs, and used to come to office every morning, after gnawing through the rope with which its master's dog-keeper endeavoured to prevent its straying. Kipling was absurdly devoted to 'Vic', and she appears and reappears, often under her own name, in many of his stories. She was a dog with many human points, and an entertaining companion. Her breed too was reputed excellent, but she looked wonderfully like a nice clean suckling pig.

Journalism in India is uncommonly hard labour for the few Englishmen who constitute an editorial staff; and with the greatest dislike of using a razor to cut grindstones, I could not help burdening Kipling with a good deal of daily drudgery. My experience of him as a newspaper hack suggests, however, that if you want to find a man who will cheerfully do the office work of three men, you should catch a young genius. Like a blood horse between the shafts of a coal-wagon, he may go near to bursting his heart in the effort, but he'll drag that wagon along as it ought to go. The amount of 'stuff' that Kipling got through in the day was indeed wonderful; and though I had more or less satisfactory assistants after he left, and the staff grew with the paper's prosperity, I am sure that more solid work was done in that office when Kipling and I worked together than ever before or after.

There was one peculiarity of Kipling's work which I really must mention; namely, the amount of ink he used to throw about. In the heat of summer white cotton trousers and thin vest constituted his office attire, and by the day's end he was spotted all over like a

Dalmatian dog. He had a habit of dipping his pen frequently and deep into the ink-pot, and as all his movements were abrupt, almost jerky, the ink used to fly. When he darted into my room, as he used to do about one thing or another in connection with the contents of the paper a dozen times in the morning I had to shout to him to 'stand off'; otherwise, as I knew by experience, the abrupt halt he would make, and the flourish with which he placed the proof in his hand before me, would send the penful of ink – he always had a *full* pen in his hand – flying over me. Driving or sometimes walking home to breakfast in his light attire plentifully besprinkled with ink, his spectacled face peeping out under an enormous, mushroom-shaped pith hat, Kipling was a quaint-looking object. This was in the hot weather, when Lahore lay blistering month after month under the sun, and every white woman and half of the white men had fled to cooler altitudes in the Himalayas, and only those men were left who, like Kipling and myself, *had* to stay. So it mattered little in what costume we went to and from the office. In the winter, when 'society' had returned to Lahore, Kipling was rather scrupulous in the matter of dress, but his lavishness in the matter of ink changed not with the seasons.

He was always the best of good company, bubbling over with delightful humour, which found vent in every detail of our day's work together; and the chance visitor to the Editor's office must often have carried away very erroneous notions of the amount of work which was being done when he found us in the fits of laughter that usually accompanied our consultations about the make-up of the paper. This is my chief recollection of Kipling as assistant and companion. And I would place sensitiveness as his second characteristic. Although a master of repartee, for instance, he dreaded dining at the Club, where there was one resident member who disliked him and was always endeavouring to snub him. Kipling's retorts invariably turned the tables on his assailant and set us all in a roar; and, beside this, Kipling was popular in the Club, while the other was not. Under such circumstances, an ordinary man would have courted the combat and enjoyed provoking his clumsy opponent. But the man's animosity hurt Kipling, and I knew that he often, to avoid the ordeal, dined in solitude at home when he would infinitely have preferred dining with me at the Club.

For a mind thus highly strung the plains of India in the hot weather make a bad abiding-place; and many of Kipling's occasional verses and passages in the Indian stories tell us how deep he drank at times of the bitterness of the dry cup that rises to the lips of the Englishman in India in the scorching heat of the sleepless Indian night. In the dregs of that cup lies madness; and the keener the intellect, and the more tense the sensibilities, the greater the danger. I suffered little in the hot weather, day or night; and yet Kipling, who suffered much at times, willingly went through trials in pursuit of his art which nothing would have induced me to undergo. His 'City of Dreadful Night'[4] was no fancy sketch, but a picture burned into his brain during the suffocating night-hours that he spent exploring the reeking dens of opium and vice in the worst quarters of the native city of Lahore; while his 'City of Two Creeds'[5] was another picture of Lahore from the life–and the death– when he watched Mussulman and Hindu spending the midnight hours in mutual butchery.

While possessing a marvellous faculty for assimilating local colour without apparent effort, Kipling neglected no chance and spared no labour in acquiring experience that might serve a literary purpose. Of the various races of India, whom the ordinary Englishman lumps together as 'natives', Kipling knew the quaintest details respecting habits, language, and distinctive ways of thought. I remember well one long-limbed Pathan, indescribably filthy, but with magnificent mien and features–Mahbub Ali,[6] I think, was his name–who regarded Kipling as a man apart from all other 'sahibs'. After each of his wanderings across the unexplored fringes of Afghanistan, where his restless spirit of adventure led him, Mahbub Ali always used to turn up travel-stained, dirtier and more majestic than ever, for confidential colloquy with 'Kuppeleen Sahib', his 'friend'; and I more than fancy that to Mahbub Ali, Kipling owed the wonderful local colour which he was able to put into the story of 'The Man Who Would Be King'.

And Mahbub Ali, peace to his ashes, was only one link in the strange chain of associations that Kipling riveted round himself in India. No half-note in the wide gamut of native ideas and custom was unfamiliar to him: just as he had left no phase of white life in India unexplored. He knew the undercurrent of the soldier's thoughts, in the whitewashed barracks on the sunburnt plain of Mian Mir, better than sergeant or chaplain. No father confessor penetrated more deeply into the thoughts of fair but frail humanity than Kipling, when the frivolous society of Anglo-India formed the object of his inquiries. The 'railway folk', that queer colony of white, half white and three-quarters black, which remains an uncared-for

and discreditable excrescence upon British rule in India, seemed to
have unburdened their souls to Kipling of all their grievances, their
poor pride, and their hopes. Some of the best of Kipling's work is
drawn from the lives of these people; although to the ordinary
Anglo-Indian, whose social caste restrictions are almost more
inexorable than those of the Hindu whom he affects to despise on
that account, they are as a sealed book. Sometimes, taking a higher
flight, Kipling has made viceroys and commanders-in-chief, members of Council and secretaries to Government his theme, and the
flashes of light that he has thrown upon the inner workings of the
machinery of government in India have been recognised as too truly
coloured to be intuitive or aught but the light of knowledge reflected
from the actual facts. No writer, for instance, could have excited, as
Kipling did, Lord Dufferin's curiosity as to how the inmost councils
of the State had thus been photographed, without having somehow
or other caught a glimpse of things as they were for at least one
moment. It is this which is the strongest attribute of Kilping's mind:
that it photographs, as it were, every detail of passing scenes that can
have any future utility for literary reference or allusion. He was
able, however he might be engaged, to make mental excursions of
various kinds while still pursuing the even tenor of the business in
hand.

In sporting matters, for instance, I suppose nothing is more
difficult than for a man who is no 'sportsman'—in the exclusive
sense of the men who carry the scent of the stables and the sawdust of
the ring with them wherever they go—to speak to these in their own
language, along their own lines of thought. Of a novelist who writes
a good sporting story, it is considered praise to say that 'none but a
real sportsman could have written it'. But Kipling was no sportsman
and an indifferent horseman; yet his sporting verses always took the
sporting world in India (where sport takes precedence of almost
every other form of human activity) by storm. I recollect in
particular one case, in which a British cavalry regiment, once
famous in the annals of sport and quartered at Umballa,[7] formerly
renowned as the headquarters of military steeplechasing in India,
published an advertisement of their steeplechases and, to attract
number rather than quality of entries, stated that the fences were
'well sloped' and 'littered on the landing side,'[8] or something to that
effect. Now, if Kipling had ridden a steeplechase then, I imagine the
odds would have been against his and the horse's arriving at the
winning post together. In India he could only have seen a few

second-class steeplechases in the way that the ordinary spectator sees them. But he wrote a poem upon this advertisement, reminding the regiment of what they had been, and of what Umballa had once been, in sport, and filled with such technicalities of racing and stable jargon that old steeplechasers went humming it all over every station in upper India and swearing that it was the best thing ever written in English. It was a bitter satire on the degeneracy in sport of the cavalry officers who 'sloped' and 'littered' their fences to make the course easy and safe. To the non-sporting reader the technical words gave good local colour, and might or might not have been rightly used. But what impressed me was that a sporting 'vet', who had lived in the pigskin almost all his life, should have gone wandering about the Lahore Club asking people, 'Where does the youngster pick it all up?' As for the bitterness of the satire, it is enough to say that, many years after, an officer of the regiment, finding the verses in the scrap-book of a friend in whose house he was staying, apologised for the necessity of tearing the page out and burning it.

It was to Kipling's powers of satire, indeed, that his early fame in India was mainly due. The poems that made up his *Departmental Ditties*[9] were personal and topical in their origin, and gained tenfold in force for readers who could supply the names and places. There have been Davids and Uriahs in all ages and countries; and the poem 'Jack Barrett[10] Went to Quetta' may be taken as applicable to all. But those who had known the real 'Jack Barrett', good fellow that he was, and the vile superior and faithless wife who sent him 'on duty' to his death, felt the heat of the spirit which inspired Kipling's verse in a way that gave those few lines an imperishable force. 'Jack Barrett' was the type of Kipling's most successful earlier verse. His short stories of frivolous anglo-Indian society are equally true to life. The lighthearted, or rather heartless, *amours* of Simla must have been witnessed at close range if one would thoroughly appreciate Kipling's picturesque travesties of the wiles and the wooings of Mrs Hauksbee and the rest. Everyone in northern India knew who these ladies were; and the knowledge gave a particular interest to the *Plain Tales from the Hills*. As an instance of Simla 'local colour', I might note the one phrase of 'black-and-yellow wasps'. All wasps are black and yellow – at least all English wasps are – but those who knew Simla when Kipling wrote of it would recollect that *the* social 'wasp' of Simla society, the original 'Mrs Hauksbee', in fact, used to be conspicuous at the dances at Viceregal Lodge for the magnificent costumes of black and yellow with which she draped her slim-waisted figure.

Kipling took life as it came, generally with merriment; and every evening during the 'season', dressed as to gloves etc. with rather scrupulous care for India, where considerable latitude in social costume prevails, he might have been seen, mounted on a swish-tailed chestnut Arab – with 'which he never established fully confidential relations – trotting along the 'Mall', as the chief road in up-country Indian stations is called, to the 'Hall', where 'society' forgathered.

One day when we were dressing in the morning, I heard Kipling shouting and went into his room. His face was pale with horror, and he was tightly clasping one leg above the knee. 'There's a snake', he gasped, 'inside my trousers, and I think I've got him by the head. Put your hand up from below and drag him out.' I observed that Kipling only 'thought' he had it by the head, and that its head might be at the other end, in which case – but, before I had finished, I saw the horror in his face relax and give place to a puzzled look, succeeded by fits of laughter. Endeavouring to ascertain by the sense of touch whether it was the head he was grasping, he discovered that it did not really feel like any part of a snake at all. In fact it had a buckle; and he realised that his braces had been dangling inside the garment when he put it on! But the danger of snakes in Lahore was real enough, and the place was rich in scorpions. I had been stung by a scorpion in bed one morning and Kipling aided me in the afternoon in a scorpion-hunt. We found twenty-six under the matting in the verandah outside my bedroom door, besides a few centipedes; and we put the lot into a large tumbler and filled it up with whisky. Wasps may also be almost classed among the dangers of Anglo-Indian life in the Punjab. Fatal results occasionally result from their stings, and they swarm everywhere; so Kipling and I waged war upon the wasps which studded the 'farash'[11] trees outside the house with their untidy nests. Other of our researches into natural history concerned 'Obadiah',[12] a tame crow which we had picked up in a crippled condition in the road. He became our 'Office Crow', and we had just determined to open a column in the paper for 'Caws by the Office Crow', upon politics and things in general, when Kipling was translated from Lahore to Allahabad, and left me to become assistant editor of *The Pioneer*.

For the latter paper he undertook a tour of the native states of

India, and wrote a series of humorous letters under the heading 'Letters of Marque',[13] republished (without Kipling's consent) in volume form. Several incidents in his travels in some of the native states showed that he possessed considerable resource and physical courage: a fact which was not new to me, for in the course of his duties as assistant editor at Lahore, he once had to engage in bodily combat with an irate and inebriated photographer who invaded the office, and, in spite of the superior bulk of his enemy, Kipling emerged from the struggle triumphant. On another occasion I recollect a convivial party of about a dozen men about to separate in the small hours of the morning, when someone suggested 'drawing' Kipling, whose house was close by. They proceeded thither, and stealthily entered Kipling's sleeping-room. As a rule, when a man is thus favoured by a surprise visit from a party of his friends in the dead of night, he is at first alarmed, and afterwards effusively friendly. But Kipling was out of his bed in an instant, and before the foremost of the intruders had mastered the geography of the room in the dark, he felt the cold barrel of a revolver at his temple. This led to explanations, and as the party filed out of the house again, it did not seem as if the laugh had been on their side.

Having, to my own great delight, 'discovered' Kipling (though his name was already a household word throughout India) in 1886, I thought that the literary world at home should share my pleasure. He was just then publishing his first little book in India; but the 'Departmental Ditties' were good enough, as I thought at the time, and as afterwards turned out, to give him a place among English writers of the day. So I obtained eight copies, and distributed them, with recommendatory letters, among the editors of English journals of light and leading. So far as I could ascertain, not a single one of those papers condescended to say a word about the unpretentious little volume. It had not come, I suppose, through 'the proper channel', i.e. from the advertising publisher.

Some years later Kipling launched himself in England with several volumes, including a new edition of *Departmental Ditties*, ready for the advertising publisher. Then the advertising publisher discovered his value, and sent his books to the literary journals; the literary journals discovered his merit, and recommended him to the British public, and the British public hastened to buy his works. Out of sight of the English Press, Kipling had worked like a grub of genius, in a remote corner of the Indian Empire, spinning a golden web out of which only stray strands floated ownerless now and then into the side columns of English papers. Without in any way destroying their English copyright value, he had been able in India to publish and revise and republish his work with the aid of the criticism of the most cultured audience to which an English writer can appeal. In Anglo-India there are no uneducated readers, for 99 per cent of the men out there have passed difficult competitive examinations to get there. When he left India I often offered to bet with men out there who dissented from my estimate of his power, any amount they liked to name within my means, that before a year had passed he would be one of the most famous writers in England. None of them dissented to the extent of taking my bet, and the result justified their caution.

When I knew Kipling in India he was bubbling over with poetry, which his hard day's office work gave him no time to write. The efforts of the native police-band in the public gardens at Lahore to discourse English music to a sparse gathering of native nurses and infants would awaken, as we passed, some rhythm with accompanying words in his mind, and he would be obviously ill at ease because he could not get within reach of pen and ink. Whether Kipling would ever have been much of a musician, I cannot say; but I know that all the poems he wrote during the years we worked together – many of the 'Departmental Ditties' – for instance – were written not only *to* music, but *as* music. I have before me now one of Kipling's poems of the 'Departmental Ditty' order which was never published. One of India's 'little wars' was in progress, and our special correspondent had telegraphed that, on account of our newspaper's comments on the composition of the General's staff, he had been boycotted by the General's orders. 'Here', said I, handing the telegram to Kipling, 'is a subject for a nice little set of verses.'

Kipling read the telegram, thought a moment; then said, 'I have it. How would this do – "Rum tiddy um ti tum ti tum,Tra la la ti tum ti tum"?' (or words to that effect) hummed in notes that suggested a solo on the bugle. I was quite accustomed to having verses in their inceptional stage submitted in this shape for editorial approval; so I said that the poem sounded excellent, and returned to my work. In twenty minutes Kipling came to me with the verses, which commenced,

> General Sir Arthur Victorius Jones,
> Great is vermilion splashed with gold.

They were pointed and scathing; but, as I have said, were never published, subsequent telegrams showing that our correspondent had been mistaken. Kipling always conceived his verses in that way –as a tune, often a remarkably musical and, to me, novel tune. He will always do so, I fancy; because, only the other day in Vermont, I heard him read, or rather intone, some of his unpublished Barrack-Room Ballads to original tunes, which were infinitely preferable to the commonplace melodies to which his published ballads have been unworthily set – with the exception, perhaps, of 'Mandalay'.[14] When he had got a tune into his head, the words and rhyme came as readily as when a singer vamps his own banjo accompaniment.

On the principle that scarcity enhances the value of every commodity, and that men value most what they cannot get, almost all Englishmen in India, where English ladies are comparatively few, become what are called 'ladies' men', and Kipling was never without friends of the other sex. Intellectual women, who are proportionately numerous in India, were especially fond of his society; and the witty wife of a gallant colonel still frequently boasts at Simla that the dedication of Kipling's first work,[15] 'To the Wittiest Woman in India', applies to her. General opinion, however, holds that Kipling intended the phrase for his mother, and, indeed, it might have been worse applied. Another charming woman friend of Kipling's, who is now dead, but while living was especially proud of the confidence implied in the occasional submission of his manuscript for her approval, was the wife of an Anglo-Indian novelist and verse-writer, now coming into English repute. And much of his keen insight into the working of the feminine mind was due to the acquaintance of these and other ladies, as well as to his home influence.

When Kipling first left India he kept up some sort of connection with me and the *Civil and Military Gazette* by writing occasional sketches for us. The pay he got for these was so small in proportion to the money he could make in England that I accepted them as tokens of friendship, which indeed they were, for me and 'The Rag'.

NOTES

E. Kay Robinson, the new editor of the *Civil and Military Gazette*, wanted to put 'sparkle' into his paper, and commissioned Kipling to write pieces that would be 'topical, arresting, and short, restricted to 2000 words'. These 'turnover pieces' running from p. 1 to p. 2, proved very popular, and included thirty-two of the *Plain Tales*. A good friend of the Lockwood Kiplings, Kay Robinson encouraged

Rudyard to try for literary success in London.

1. A beautiful, talented American actress (1859–1940), who was very popular in England from 1883 on.

2. The Christmas annual of the *Civil and Military Gazette*, written by Kipling, his father, mother and sister, and first appearing in 1885 at Lahore.

3. A province in what today is Pakistan.

4. Originally a poem by James Thomson, published in the *National Reformer* (1874); later used as a title by Kipling (1890) to depict Lahore, sweltering under intense heat during the July rains; collected in *Life's Handicap* as the twenty-fourth title.

5. Printed in *Civil and Military Gazette*, 19 and 20 Oct 1885; not collected.

6. An Afghan horse-dealer, one of the main characters in *Kim*.

7. A city and district in Punjab, British India; today, a town of the Punjab state in India.

8. Steeplechasing requires that there be at least one ditch and six birch-fences 4 feet 6 inches high for every mile; the hurdles, packed with gorse and slightly sloped, must be not less than 3 feet 6 inches from bottom bar to top bar (*Oxford Companion to Sports and Games*).

9. A series of humorous poems about Anglo-Indian life, published in Calcutta in 1886.

10. In 'The Story of Uriah' (first printed in the *Civil and Military Gazette*, 3 Mar 1886, and collected in *Departmental Ditties and Other Verses*, 1886), Jack Barrett is a soldier sent to Quetta in September, 'and it killed him out of hand' before he drew his next month's pay. Kipling suggests that Mrs Barrett, left behind in Quetta, did not mourn long or sincerely for her husband, who had been transferred by Jack's superior officer in order to take up with her once Jack was out of the way.

11. Obsolete form of 'ferash', which denotes a menial servant whose proper business is to spread carpets, pitch tents, and perform similar domestic work.

12. Minor prophet. Shortest book in the Old Testament. The name means 'servant of Yah (weh)'.

13. Nineteen sketches about a month of loaferdom in Rajputana (Nov–Dec 1887), sent home to Kipling's paper at Allahabad.

14. A ballad first published in the *Scots Observer*, 21 June 1890; collected in *Departmental Ditties, Barrack-Room Ballads and Other Verses* (1890).

15. *Plain Tales from the Hills* was published in India in 1888, but prior to that year Kipling had already published several 'books'; see James McG. Stewart, *Rudyard Kipling: A Bibliographical Catalogue*, ed. A. W. Yeats (Toronto: Dalhousie University Press and University of Toronto Press, 1959) pp. 3–28.

Rudyard Kipling as Journalist*

E. KAY ROBINSON

From his father Rudyard Kipling has inherited the artistic tendency which leads him to fill any odd scrap of paper near his hand with some grotesque sketch of the incident or idea uppermost in his mind. Quaint and uncanny faces almost always adorned the edges of his writing-blocks in the newspaper-office at Lahore, and many hundreds of drawings which the autograph-hunter would now value have gone the way of the waste-paper basket. He illustrated, too, the connection between music and poetry in the fact that before composing verses he hummed a tune to fit them to, and in reading his finished verses he delivers them, sometimes at any rate, in recitative. The thought may be worth following up how far the conjunctions of sketching with prose and singing with poetry suggest the natural relations of those arts to literature. . . .

That trick of wiping his spectacles is one which Kipling indulges more frequently than any man I have ever met, for the simple reason that he is always laughing; and when you laugh till you nearly cry your glasses get misty. Kipling, shaking all over with laughter and wiping his spectacles at the same time with his handkerchief, is the picture which always comes to mind as most characteristic of him in the old days when even our hardest work on 'The Rag'—for fate soon took me to Lahore to be his editor—was as full of jokes as a pomegranate of pips. The 'high-collar' days, when there were no telegrams, and editorial matter had to be forthcoming to fill the space right up to the top of the columns; the 'patent seamless' leader of emergency; the 'stringing' of selected extracts;

* *Literature*, IV (18 Mar 1899) 285–6.

the fitting of 'whip-lashes' to notes; and the manufacture of 'scraps' all gave a mixed bag of sport; but the ecstasy of literary composition was reached in the joint composition of repartees to the attacks of our dear contemporaries.

There was one Anglo-Indian magazine which arrogated to its second-rate self the title of the *Cream of Reviews*,[1] and for reasons which do not matter it fell foul of 'The Rag'–by which affectionate title we knew our own *Civil and Military Gazette*. So we put our heads together and concocted an article 'Concerning Some Sour Cream', which moved the enemy to wrath so nearly speechless that in its next issue it refused to argue further with a 'hireling organ which shoots out its wooden head and mocks'. 'Shoot out your wooden head and mock!' became thenceforth the office exhortation whenever there was journalistic warfare toward, which was often: for 'The Rag' was distinctly militant in those days. 'Longs and Shorts' was another merry jape; but of all journalistic feats we had most reason to be proud of our earthquake.

This earthquake occurred at about 2.30 a.m. one Sunday morning. In those days the Saturday paper, dated Monday, according to Anglo-Indian practice–for at the stations the native newsboys offer you always 'Tomorrow's paper, Sahib' – used to go to press in the small hours of Sunday morning to catch the Bombay and Calcutta mail trains. It was always practically finished by midnight, and only one page remained 'open' for telegrams. On this occasion we had spent the hours from midnight till half-past two at the club, which was emptied by that time of revellers, and returned to the bungalow, when we both noticed a slight tremor as of an earthquake. To verify the matter we looked at a hanging hook on a door; yes, it was swinging, so in went a brief paragraph in the paper, among the very latest news, announcing a 'slight earthquake' at Lahore. Not another soul in Lahore or in any part of the Punjab or India felt that earthquake, and the Government observatory knew nothing of it. It was our own private and special earthquake, and we treasure its memory. After the last English earthquake, he wrote to me,

This here English journalism isn't what it's cracked up to be. They can't have an earthquake in England without taking up two cols of *The Times* to describe the effects and to verify the direction and nature of the shock. This does not give scope for invention. Now, I remember the time when you and I could just make an earthquake, same as the Almighty, slip it into the 'local' at 3 a.m. of a Sunday morning, and go to bed with the consciousness we'd done our duty by the proprietors. Wonder what they'd say on the *Globe* to so strictly local an earthquake as ours?

Surprise is generally expressed at the mastery possessed by Kipling of the technicalities of so many professions. As a rule the soldier, sailor, sportsman, engineer, or naturalist will detect the erring hand of the lay writer in almost every paragraph; but the peculiarity of Rudyard Kipling's work is that just when it is most technical it appeals most strongly to the admition of the men with whose craft it deals. Many regard the power as an almost uncanny adjunct of his genius. Yet it is in truth the result of the most prosaic of all the attributes of genius – namely, the infinite capacity for taking pains. To learn to write as soldiers think he spent long hours loafing with the genuine article. He watched them at work and at play and at prayer from the points of view of all his confidants – the combatant officer, the doctor, the chaplain, the drill sergeant, and the private himself. With the Navy, with every branch of sport and with natural history, he has never wearied in seeking to learn all that man may learn at first-hand, or the very best second-hand, at any rate. Hence he can write of Esquimaux as though he had lived for years among them, and of the jungle beasts in the very echoes of the jungle. But most wonderful is his insight into the strangely mixed manners of life and thought of the natives of India. He knew them all through their horizontal divisions of rank and their vertical sections of caste; their ramifications of race and blood; their antagonisms and blendings of creed; and their hereditary streaks of calling or handicraft. Show him a native, and he would tell you his rank, caste, race, origin, habitat, creed, and calling. He would speak to the man in his own fashion, using familiar, homely figures which brightened the other's surprised eyes with recognition of brotherhood and opened a straight way into his confidence. In two minutes the man – perhaps a wild hawk from the Afghan hills – would be pouring out into the ear of this sahib with heaven-sent knowledge and sympathy the weird tale of the blood-feud and litigation, the border fray, and the usurer's iniquity, which had driven him so far afield as Lahore from Bajaur.[2] To Kipling even the most suspected and suspicious of classes, the religious mendicants, would open their mouths freely.

By the road, thick with the dust of camels and thousands of cattle and goats, which winds from Lahore Fort across the River Ravi, there are walled caravanserais, the distant smell of which more than suffices for most of the Europeans who pass; but sitting with the travellers from Bokhara[3] or Badakshan,[4] in the reeking interior Kipling heard weird tales and gathered much knowledge. Under a spreading peepul tree overhanging a well by the same road squatted daily a ring of almost naked fakirs, smeared with ashes, who scowled at the European driving by, but for Kipling there was, if he wished it, an opening in the squatting circle and much to be learned from the unsavoury talkers. That is how his finished word-pictures take the lifelike aspect of instantaneous photographs. When, moreover, any man acquired a reputation for special skill in his calling, to him Kipling always went for knowledge. From men like Warburton of the Police,[5] J. R. Bell of the Civil Engineers, Mulroney of the Medical, Henderson of the Secret Service, and others – mostly dead now – he learned the secrets of life and work and crime on the large and often lurid scale that fits the colouring of an Eastern canvas.

That Kipling, given health and strength, will return to India I am sure. His pen is a magnet to draw him thither; and, as he has already done once since fame was his, he will sit again in a chair in the office of the old Rag, ask after the old native hands by name, and try to recall the aroma of the days when the waste-paper basket under the editor's table used to receive some of his rejected MSS. It is not fashionable to reject Kipling's MSS now.

NOTES

1. An unsigned article, 'Concerning Some Sour Cream', appeared in the *Civil and Military Gazette* on 31 August, 1886. The author was probably Kipling. It was a counter-attack on an article by Thomas Edwards, printed in the periodical *Cream*, which had criticised statements made in *The Pioneer*. The invective was so whoopingly enthusiastic that Kipling, who never collected it, may have regretted having written it.

2. Pathan in the Afghan–Pakistan frontier region. A member of the Bajouri people.

3. Capital of the region in the Uzbek Soviet Socialist Republic. Located on the old silk-trade route between Europe and China.

4. A plateau in Afghanistan, north of the main ridge of the watershed between the Helmand and the Indus basins.

5. Sir Robert Warburton (1842–99) was the son of Robert Warburton of the Royal Artillery and a noble Afghan lady. He served mainly on the frontier; had a remarkable influence on the hill tribes; and was called 'warden of the Khyber'. He wrote *Eighteen Years in the Khyber* (1900).

Mr Kipling as Journalist*

E. KAY ROBINSON

Kipling has said that he who has once been a journalist remains a journalist to the end. He said this in a semi-autobiographical sense. But when a man has reached the point of having it even rumoured that syndicates are formed to buy his manuscripts at the rate of so much a word the mill of daily journalism must go round without him.

But once Kipling was a journalist to the marrow; and there was real pathos in his parting with the 'rag' in India which he had for years done so much to adorn. When, too, after fame was his, and America and England competed for his copy, he sent many a sketch in his best vein to the old paper at the old low rate of pay. The early hours of the first morning of his flying return visit to Lahore, his *City of Two Creeds*, saw him, for sheer love of the old work, sitting in the familiar office chair, correcting the same old proofs on the same old yellow paper, with Mian Rukn-Din, the Mohammedan foreman printer, flying round the press with green turban awry, informing all the hands that 'Kuppuleen Sahib'[1] had returned. And there his old editor found him when he came to office. But those times are not now.

Lahore, however, stands where it did. Two-and-a-half days' journey up-country from Bombay you will find the many-mosqued capital of the armed Punjab, and there on the right-hand side of the broad Mall, embowered in siris and peepul trees, behind a lawn studded with palms and Bougainvillias, whose planting Kipling helped to superintend, a large building bears across its front the legend, 'The Civil and Military Gazette Press'. There Kipling worked for years, and before that, when the *Civil and Military Gazette* was still a losing venture, he had worked for it also in humbler premises, near the native city, where the Eurasians live in dark-

*   *The Academy*, L (28 Nov 1896) 458–9.

verandahed bungalows, and where the native pleader bargains with his clients.

As a boy from school, Kipling was brought out to India, and began at once to earn his modest monthly wage at the bottom of the ladder of Anglo-Indian journalism. Newspaper work in India is carried on by three classes of men. The natives – Hindu, Mohammedan, and Sikh – labour side by side in setting up the type and working the machines. Eurasians and domiciled British subjects supply the staff of 'readers'; while the comparatively expensive, because imported, Anglo-Indians fill the editorial staff. And who are the shorthand reporters and sub-editors? In Kipling's day the up-country newspaper had none. The editorial staff, comprising two men, did the entire work of getting out the daily paper; and if you want to know how Kipling worked, as one of the two men who produced the *Civil and Military Gazette* daily, with its seven pages of reading matter and seven of advertisements, you could not do better than turn into that large double bungalow on the Lahore Mall and ask cheery Mian Rukn-Din, the Mohammedan foreman printer; ask Bhai Pertab Singh, the loyal and orthodox Sikh book-keeper; ask Babu Hakim Ali, the courteous Moslem clerk, to whom was entrusted the task of pasting Kipling's printed work into volumes – for from the earliest days Kipling had the careful habits that so seldom accompany genius such as his; ask Habibulla, the willing chaprassi [Messenger runner], on whose head Kipling's office box came and went daily. They will tell you *how* Kipling worked. As a journalist, he was the man whom all editors seek and few find. He was a staff in himself. He distrusted his own powers, it is true, so much that to demand a leading article from him filled him with anguish. He said it was 'above him'; and he scarcely wrote five in as many years. But for every other kind of work, from writing editorial 'notes' to putting side-heads to paragraphs, or reporting a police-court case, he was as willing as he was gifted. To every grade of work he brought a brilliance of happy thought which placed his topic in its brightest light, a dead-sure aim with words which made his headlines fit his matter with that complete aptness which satisfies the editorial heart; a command of abrupt turns of expression which supplied humorous side-headings to small paragraphs in such taking ways that the reader could not help but read; but more than all, he exhibited a conscientious industry and an inexhaustible pluck in his work which made his friends many times fear that the quick wheels of his mind would one day whirr and stop. He went near to it once or twice. There are nights in the Punjab when the rains are delayed and the thermometer ranges about 100 degrees day and night; when the day's waking thoughts of a busy brain twist themselves into torturing nightmares in those stifling hours that precede the dawn, and the dawn brings no relief. Such nights there were in 1887, and the English-speaking world then went near to losing Kipling before it had heard of him.

But he never slackened in his work, of which on 'high-collar' days there was more than enough. A 'high-collar' day, it may be explained, was one on which no telegrams from England were received before going to press, and editorial 'Notes of the Day' had to be written to fill the column which the telegrams should have occupied, thus bringing the editorial matter close up to the head (like a high collar) of the first column. At other times a multiplicity of telegrams crowded out so many 'Notes of the Day' that several of these, dealing with cognate subjects, had to be strung together into what Kipling called 'patent seamless' leaders. Outside contributors to papers in India nearly all belong to the civil or military services, and their contributions were often bald in style, though welcome for the information they contained. Adding the few lines of comment to qualify their contributions to be used as notes Kipling described as 'fitting on the whip-lash'; and his were always neatly tied and keen in application.

The heaviest and most distasteful burden that Kipling bore in those journalistic days was the Blue Book. At certain seasons of the year the Government of India issues a stream of official reports. This flux of Blue Books has been not inaptly compared to a swarm of white ants issuing from an old beam of wood. It is the duty of the painstaking Anglo-Indian journalist to catch these reports as they come, dissect, boil down, and serve them up with such literary garnishing as may tempt the appetite of the capricious reader. Forestry, Police, Jails, Registration, Education, Public Works, etc. – each with its pages of statistics – come as the driest of grist to the mill, and no small portion of Kipling's working hours was devoted to the grinding thereof. Even genius cannot build in marble with mere bricks; but Kipling often went near to converting Government reports into interesting and picturesque narrative. Besides this, a great deal of sub-editor's work necessarily fell to his share when the entire drudgery of the daily paper had to be done by two men. He was an adroit wielder of scissors and paste-brush, with a quick eye for matter worth republishing, and a happy knack of knocking it into shape. As a reporter, whenever the nature of the function to be described lent itself to graphic or humorous treatment, Kipling was inimitable; and brilliant fragments of the experience thus gained of viceregal durbars or 'tamashas'[2] in native states flash from the pages of many of his later sketches. But his was a very mixed bag of work. After-dinner speeches at commemorative banquets, university convocations, race-meetings or lawsuits, a flower-show or a military review, whatever came it was always Kipling's turn to 'do' it, for there was no one else but the Editor. Probably the worst job ever entrusted to Kipling was his mission to interview a notorious fakir, about whom there was great religious excitement in the Punjab, as he was reported to have cut out his tongue in order that it might, with the help of the goddess Kali,[3] grow again in six weeks, and thus prove the verity of the Hindu faith. Kipling never found the fakir; but, through a hot Indian day, he found himself misdirected from one unsavoury slum of Amritsar to another, till he was sick to death of his quest. It no doubt suited the fakir's game to be evasive when a sahib was looking for him; and on his return to Lahore it was a very dirty and travel-stained Kipling who cheerily expressed the hope that the next time the Editor wanted details of a tongue-cutting boom he would go and get them for himself.

Besides occasional reporting outside the office, Kipling's daily work on the *Civil and Military Gazette* was, briefly: (1) to prepare for press all the telegrams of the day; (2) to provide all the extracts and paragraphs; (3) to make headed articles out of official reports, etc.; (4) to write such editorial notes as he might have time for; (5) to look generally after all sports, out-station and local intelligence; (6) to read all proofs except the editorial matter. He may have had to do more; but, roughly speaking, for a few, a very few hundreds of rupees a month, he did the work of at least two men, and in his odd moments of leisure wrote his verses and sketches, some of which have been republished in *Departmental Ditties*, *Soldiers Three*, and *Plain Tales from the Hills*. These were scarcely journalism, but they were the only portion of his work which ever needed 'editing'. His youthful fancy now and then kicked too freely over the traces of convention, and more than one sketch found its home in the waste-paper basket. As a rule, however, they were much too good for a hack's pay on a paper in the north-west of India, and even Kipling's modesty, almost a fault, could not blind him to the fact that he was selling his brain-work far below its market value, wasting its razor edge on blocks of literally worthless and perishable matter; but he believed that he owed a debt of gratitude to the newspaper proprietors who took him on credit and gave him a salary when he was a boy fresh from school, and he determined to serve them loyally for a full term of years.

NOTES

1. A Moslem's pronunciation of 'Kipling'.
2. An entertainment or show, display, or public function (an Urdu word).
3. Hindu goddess, also called Durga. Mentioned in 'The Miracle of Purun Bhagat', and several other Kipling stories.

Kipling – Some Recollections*

MICHAEL O'DWYER

It is almost exactly fifty years since I made the acquaintance of Kipling in the old Punjab Club at Lahore.

He was then twenty, and for two years had been working as assistant editor of the *Civil and Military Gazette*, the organ of the British community in north-west India. I was a year older and had just come out in the ICS.[1]

I last met Kipling a few months ago at the Athenaeum of which we were fellow members, and where, after I returned from India in 1920, we had many talks over the old days in the Punjab.

Kipling's father was, in 1886, Principal of the School of Art in Lahore where he did splendid work in keeping alive the old indigenous arts and crafts.

The Kipling family, including Mrs Kipling, a lady of great charm and culture, and their son Rudyard and daughter Beatrice, an attractive and gifted girl, played a great part in the social and intellectual life of Lahore, which was then a dingy dusty provincial capital, well described in 'The Chronicles of Dustypore'.

* *Saturday Review*, CLXI (25 Jan 1936) 105–6.

But I doubt if we young Philistines, deeply immersed in our own work, realised at the start the genius of young Kipling, though his biting wit and ready repartee often amused and sometimes lacerated us.

Between 1886 and 1889, the results of his marvellous intuition into characters the most complex and diverse and of his unerring accuracy of observation were made public in what were then regarded as amusing *jeux d'esprit* or *vers d'occasion* such as *Departmental Ditties, Plain Tales from the Hills*, and *Soldiers Three*.

These and other short stories appeared as 'turnovers' in the *Civil and Military Gazette*. The first two lashed with bitter satire the follies and frivolities of Anglo-Indian and especially Simla society; the third, which became almost as famous as *The Three Musketeers*, gave an inimitable picture of the types – Mulvaney, Learoyd and Ortheris – that went to make up the British Tommy of those days.

That fine regiment the 5th Fusiliers (the Fighting Fifth) was then quartered at Lahore Cantonment, and Kipling, with characteristic thoroughness, went to the fountain-head – the Sergeants' Mess and the regimental canteen – for his characters.

But even in those early years his mind was working on the super problems of India. He saw far below the surface and also far into the future; his forecasts in 'What Happened' and 'The White Man's Burden', of what the then nascent Congress Movement would lead to in a generation showing prophetic vision.

Kipling left India for good in 1889, but some of his best work on Indian subjects, notably the incomparable *Kim*, were written later.

I saw nothing of him till I returned from India in 1920. But at Lahore in 1917 I had the pleasure as Lieutenant Governor of unveiling a tablet to him in the office-room of the *Civil and Military Gazette*, where he had worked for four years and established his youthful reputation.

When we met again in 1920 he was delighted to hear all about his old haunts and friends and said to me with pride 'In that paper I was fifty–fifty.'

His accurate recollection and knowledge of Indian affairs with which he had no direct contact for over thirty years were phenomenal.

As might be expected from the poet of our empire he lamented the steady surrender of our position and responsibilities in India, having little faith in 'Pagett, MP'[2] and still less in the capacity of the Indian intelligentsia to govern with the pen and the tongue martial peoples who regarded those weapons with distrust or disdain.

More than once in recent years I urged him to come forward and expose the dangers of the policy of surrender, arguing that his name and authority would compel people to think.

His reply was to this effect: 'I have been forty years before my time in uttering the warning. For over thirty years I have been trying to hammer into the heads of certain British public men the elementary facts about India. I have had no success.'

When I asked him to try the Press he flashed out the caustic retort, 'The Press is doped or roped.'

He was sore at heart in contemplating the surrender of so much that the British in India had stood for and that he had glorified in his writings.

But a few years ago I persuaded him to join the Indian Defence League,[3] and he was made one of the vice-presidents.

He then told me he was meditating whether to come out into the open and was collecting material for the purpose, but this never came to realisation.

He doubtless thought that nothing could prevail against a subservient majority in Parliament and a 'doped' Press as he put it.

As an instance of his political foresight, I may quote a sentence from what he wrote over thirty years ago: 'Asia is not going to be civilised after the methods of the West. There is too much Asia and she is too old. . . . . She will never attend Sunday School or learn to vote, unless she uses swords for voting tickets.'

I may close with an anecdote which brings out Kipling's modesty and filial regard.

He disliked discussing his books. But a few years ago I tackled him at the Club saying, 'Now Kipling, we all have a great admiration for your prose and your poetry. They have often been an inspiration to me and others in our strenuous but thankless task in India. But there's one thing I'd like to tell you. You never wrote as good prose as your father.'

Kipling jumped up, slapped me on the back saying, 'My dear fellow, you are one of the few people who discovered that truth. How did you do it?'

I laughingly replied, 'Because in 1888 I collaborated with your father in preparing a monograph on the woodcraft of the Punjab.'

That was only true in part, for I had only prepared the data, and the literary and descriptive part was exclusively Lockwood Kipling's. But the work of the latter which I had in mind was *Beast and Man in India*, published nearly fifty years ago and delightfully illustrated by the author.

In Kipling a great genius and a great patriot has passed away. May he rest in peace!

NOTES

Sir Michael Francis O'Dwyer (1864–1940) joined the Indian Civil Service in 1885, and was posted to the Punjab. Lord Curzon gave him heavy responsibilities for organising the new North-west Frontier Provinces. Later he served as Governor General in Central India (1910–12), and as Lieutenant Governor of the Punjab (1913–19). He was implicated in the tragic Amritsar Massacre, since he had approved General Dyer's action (1919), but an inquiry subsequently cleared him, and General Dyer was asked to resign. At the end of a crowded meeting of the Royal Central Asian Society in London (1940), an Indian assassinated him, and was captured and convicted. O'Dwyer always believed in the benefits of British rule in India.

1. The chief of the British Indian services was technically known as the Indian Civil Service. It was limited to about a thousand members at this time; they were chosen by open competition in England, and their ages were between twenty-one and twenty-four.

2. First printed in *The Pioneer*, 16 June 1886; collected in *Departmental Ditties and Other Verses* (1886).

3. The India Defence Committee was formed in March 1933; organised a demonstration at Albert Hall that was addressed by Lord Lloyd and Winston Churchill; reaffirmed faith in Conservative principles and called on the Government to abandon the India Bill, which (the Committee claimed) would put the helpless people of India back under the tyranny of the Brahmin oligarchy, and create general unrest throughout the Empire.

My Friend – Rudyard Kipling*

EDMONIA HILL

Marrying a distinguished professor in Allahabad University in the late eighties, I went to India as a bride. My domestic experiences

* *The Classmate*, XLV (17 Sep 1938) p. 7.

and social life were recorded in letters I wrote to my friends and my college paper. Chief among my pleasurable recollections is the friendship my husband and I formed with the rising young author, Rudyard Kipling.

We had been invited to dine with the Allens, who were neighbours. Mr Allen was proprietor of the Allahabad *Pioneer* and the *Civil and Military Gazette* of Lahore. *The Pioneer* was a newspaper of great interest to all Government officials, with its news of everything important for an Anglo-Indian exile to know; sailings, promotions, telegrams, foreign correspondence, local items. Its appearance was a daily event in a world so far removed from Europe as was India in the eighties and nineties.

Some very interesting articles had been appearing in *The Pioneer* entitled 'Letters of Marque', which were unsigned. We were all wondering as to their author, evidently from the Punjab. When we were seated at the table and conversation was in full swing, my partner called my attention to a short, dark-haired and moustached man of uncertain age, wearing very thick glasses. He said, 'That is Rudyard Kipling, who has just come from Lahore to be on the staff of the *Pi*. He is the writer of those charming sketches of the native states.' Of course I was at once interested.

After dinner, when the men joined the ladies in the drawing-room, the young author, who had evidently marked me as an American, and perhaps seeking copy, came to the fireplace where I was standing and began questioning me about my homeland. We became lifelong friends. My husband and I greatly enjoyed the brilliant young man. All through the years his letters came telling of his wanderings, of a new book – and why it was written – or calling attention to some magazine article about to appear.

He had arrived in India at the age of sixteen and gone to Lahore, where his parents were then living. He was made Jack-of-all-trades on the *Civil and Military Gazette*. The type for the paper was set by Indians ignorant of the English language, so proof-reading was a trial to the soul. He had his troubles in the printing-office, too, for his poems and articles had to be cut to fit. The foreman used to say to him, 'Your po'try, good sir, just coming proper length today.'

His description of the Indian press room on a hot night is of a room lighted by the flickering dips, with a hurricane lantern here and there. The half-naked men who turned the presses looked picturesque in the uncertain light as they lolled against the walls and waited for their call; the presses looked mysterious and ghastly, and from the far end came the tick-tick of the type being set up by white-sheeted yawners. They carried candles and often the grease guttered onto the type. Little naked boys who had no known business in the world there, had curled up on one of the big tables and gone to sleep.

During those years in India, of which little is told in his autobiography, we often saw him in the throes of the creative impulse; we actually watched him write some of his earlier stories. I am the proud possessor of *Early Verses*.[1] A small book bound in deep maroon, with back and corners of black striped with gold, about one half inch thick, $4\frac{1}{2} \times 6$, published by Shamus Din, Bookbinder, Lahore. The inscription is as follows: 'January 1889: from Rudyard Kipling, these the first of his ventures into print.'

In March of 1890 I had a lovely surprise one afternoon. A messenger from the *Pioneer* office appeared, bringing me a book from Mr Kipling. The title of the collection was *Plain Tales from the Hills*, which had first appeared in the *Civil and Military Gazette*. There was an amusing inscription which ended with; 'Would they were worthier. That's too late – cracked pictures stand no further stippling. Forgive the faults. To Mrs Hill – from Rudyard Kipling.'

How rich a store of material he gathered during those years in India. Occasionally he introduced into his stories pictures that he acknowledged to his friends were family portraits. In *The Brushwood Boy*[2] the charming and witty mother of George was the counterpart of his mother. In *Kim* the curator of the museum was his father, J. Lockwood Kipling, who occupied that position. The elder Kipling was deeply interested in Indian legend and folklore, the author of a delightful book entitled *Man and Beast in India*.

Still another personal touch is found in the short story 'They'.[3] It was written some time after his visit to America in 1900 when he lost his beloved daughter, Josephine. His sorrow was very deep. It is possible, therefore, to connect with that heart-breaking experience the story of 'They', in which he tells of visits to an old Elizabethan haunted house. On one occasion as he sat with his hand resting on the back of a screen, he felt his hand lifted and turned over by two small hands, and a kiss imprinted in the centre of the palm. This was the little ceremony that his beloved dead daughter had observed whenever she wanted to be near him, yet saw that he was too busy to be disturbed.

When Mr Kipling was called back to *The Pioneer* the second time, he returned at the most desolate season of the year. We invited him to be our guest. Our house was a famous old bungalow which had been standing since Mutiny days when nearly every other house was destroyed. He so appreciated the privilege of staying in our home that while we were away in the hills he wrote a clever sketch for us, telling of the daily life of the household. He pictured the attractive verandah where he spent most of his leisure time, the long avenue of thick-leaved shisham[4] trees leading to the house, and many amusing incidents. I have that manuscript begun in his fine handwriting, and hurriedly scribbled toward the last.

When we started back to the United States, Rudyard suddenly decided that he would like to see something of the world before returning to England. He begged to be allowed to accompany us. He took along two black manifold books in which he planned to write his *Sea to Sea*[5] letters. He had just received *Wee Willie Winkie*,[6] with its attractive cover-design by his father. The inscription in my copy this time ended with:

> On steamer Madura
> Now rolling through a tepid sea.
> March 10th
>   to Mrs Hill from me,
> A journalist unkempt and inky,
> With all regards, Wee Willie Winkie.

When our party arrived at Beaver, Pennsylvania, Mr Kipling settled at the College, where he had a spacious bedroom, with fireplace and bath. There was a couch where he spent much time reading and meditating, but not doing much writing. He was absorbing the new experiences. The servants were puzzled by him, especially when he demanded that the barber shave him in bed. He swapped stories with the Senator and townsfolk, arousing interest wherever he went.

When we returned to India by way of England, he sailed with us on the *City of Berlin*. We remained a while in London to help establish the helpless boy, as he seemed to us, in his new quarters. Busy days were spent visiting second-hand shops to equip the rather dull, dreary rooms at Embankment Chambers, Strand. Though lonely at first, he was soon absorbed in his work, for publishers at once made demands.

NOTES

Edmonia Hill was married to S. A. Hill, a meteorologist in Government service, appointed to a science professorship at Muir Central College, Allahabad, in 1887. She came from Beaver, Pennsylvania, and was widely known by her nickname 'Ted'. She proved to be a warm-hearted friend and discerning critic. Kipling lived in the Hills' bungalow in Allahabad during his last year in India. The death of Professor Hill in India (1890), and Kipling's aborted romance with Caroline Taylor, Edmonia's younger sister (whom he met while living for two months in the house of Mrs Hill's parents in Beaver), converted the relationship to a more formal and distant affair. Nevertheless, Edmonia was Kipling's closest confidante in the late 1880s.

1. *Echoes, by Two Writers;* see James McG. Stewart, *Rudyard Kipling: A Bibliographical Catalogue*, ed. A. W. Yeats (Toronto: Dalhousie University Press and University of Toronto Press, 1959) p. 13, for a description of this specific copy. Later, Kipling reprinted thirty-two of the thirty-nine poems of *Echoes* as his own in *Early Verse* (Outward Bound Edition, XVII; Edition de Luxe, XVIII). The other seven poems were by his sister Alice ('Trix').

2. First printed in *Century Magazine*, Dec 1895; collected in *The Day's Work* (1898).

3. First printed in *Scribner's Magazine*, Aug 1904; collected in *Traffics and Discoveries*, 1904.

4. A tall tree (sometimes 80 feet high). Considered in India to be one of the best timbers for both elasticity and durability.

5. *From Sea to Sea*, a two-volume collection of stories, sketches, and letters, was published in the United States in 1899, and in England in 1900.

6. *Wee Willie Winkie and Other Child Stories* was published in Allahabad by A. H. Wheeler and Co. in 1888.

The Young Kipling*

EDMONIA HILL

In the latter part of the nineteenth century an American girl married an Englishman who had been appointed by Lord Salisbury to fill the chair of Science at the Muir Central College,[1] Allahabad University, at Allahabad, India. The following are extracts from her diary and from letters written to her home people. . . .

* *Atlantic Monthly*, CLVII (Apr 1936) 406–15.

January 1888. Dear People: We give a garden party tomorrow. I never saw more perfect turf. About twenty old women have been squatting down picking out each stray weed and bottling it, while Umar the head gardener looks on. There are two fine tennis-courts and six badminton-courts where we can accommodate six or eight players at each. A badminton-court is smaller than a tennis-court, the net being narrower and higher. The game is played with racquet and feathered cork and is a very merry one with good players who keep the shuttlecock over the net with many rallies. The place will look very festive with the daintily gowned women, the sporting subalterns, the serious civilians, the bountifully spread tables, and the attentive servants in their picturesque uniforms and white turbans.

We sent a note to Rudyard Kipling inviting him to come to the garden party. He replied in a characteristic note saying that the tongue of Pennsylvania was the one language he long and ardently had desired to learn. He would be late, as he had to help put a paper to bed. He does not play tennis, but is quite good at badminton. He said he was pleased to come, and if life here was to be tempered with Allahabadminton he would begin to take comfort. He has told us much of his early life at school. . . .

April. I shall never forget the glee in which RK came in one afternoon saying, 'What do you suppose I just came across in reading the proof of this week's English letter? Andrew Lang[2] says, "Who is Mr Rudyard Kipling?" ' He was so pleased that they really had heard of him in England, for in all modesty he intends to make his mark in the world. . . .

One of Rudyard's stories, 'The Recrudescence of Imray',[3] had its origin in an incident at our home. There was a strange odour in the dining-room, and by luncheon-time it had become stronger and later was unbearable. As the ceilings are made of cloth to give an air-chamber to cool the room, the thatch-man was called, and upon investigation he discovered that a wee squirrel had died under the roof. R studied a while and then exclaimed, 'I have it', and the result was that terrible story of the sudden disappearance of Imray, whose body sagged on the ceiling-cloth and finally tumbled down on the table. His own servant had killed him because he had called his child handsome, thus casting the evil eye on him. After I came to India one of the first things I learned was to say to a mother, in order to warn off the evil eye, 'What an ugly child you have', no matter how winning the infant.

16 April. Dear M: Rudyard was called from Allahabad to Lahore to edit the *Civil and Military Gazette*, so he sent us a letter expressing the great joy he has at being among his own people once more, but with sadness at the many changes. He tells of being gummed into an office chair from eight in the morning till six at night, and how he has to work after dinner with nothing in the wide world to show for it except an indigestible paper which most people throw down with the genial remark, 'Oh, nothing in the *Civil and Military* as usual.'

How Kipling does love those wild men of the North! He calls them his own folk. They are savage, boastful, arrogant, and hot-headed, and these vagrant loafers, snaky-lipped and vulture-eyed, come to pay their respects to him. . . .

How I do wish you might meet this interesting man!

The outcome of his being with these Ishmaelites in North India is his tale 'Dray Wara Yow Dee'[4] and he says the incident of the killing is bodily cribbed from a frontier murder-case deposition.

I am quite flattered. RK writes that he spent the afternoon alternately browsing over a pipe and trying to hack out a *causerie intime*[5] between two girls at Simla. Because he finds it is very difficult to get the hang of conversation between girls, he asks me on some idle afternoon to look over and check the thing, as he hasn't a single sympathetic soul there to discuss things with and he is choked up with a half-dozen plans and outlines of stories. The proof came with a very wide margin for my corrections. I was gullible enough to criticise what he had written. Today he replies that he has laughed a great deal at my verdict. I do not approve of much that he writes and I'm not backward in saying so – but he goes on just the same, maligning us. He calls the story 'Poor Dear Mamma' and it is about two girls discussing a dance. One of them is in love with a man who is devoting himself to her mother. The conversation is very amusing.

Why Mr Kipling is the recipient of many a confession I never can see, as he makes use of every item for his work that he can glean. This was clearly shown once when he was at the Lahore Club. A friend came in bubbling over with newly found love. R sat at a table idly playing with a pencil. In reality he was taking down word for word what this gallant captain was saying – thoroughly enjoying his subtlety, for he intended to use every expression and he did that very thing, first as a story for *The Week's News*[6] and then combined with other tales which made up *The Story of the Gadsbys*.[7]

Mussoorie,[8] *May.* Rudyard Kipling has arrived to stay at the Charleville Hotel for a few days. He feels that he is condescending, as this is not a fashionable place and his heart is at Simla, the seat of Government, where he meets worthwhile people, grist for his writing. However, he can go nowhere in the Himalaya Mountains where he will get a better view of the snows. He is the most susceptible person I ever knew. As he came up the winding road he glimpsed a girl's head in a window, 'a golden-haired beauty', and he has been talking about her ever since. I think I know her, so I hope they can meet at a dance. Otherwise I don't see how we shall entertain him. He is full of notions and plans for his *Soldier Stories*.[9] Learoyd with his Yorkshire dialect is beyond me, though he tries to explain.

June. Rudyard is called back to *The Pioneer*, and we are discussing whether we should generously offer to take him in to our house for a little while rather than to let him go to the Club in this desolate season. He has his own trap – the 'pig and Whistle', as he calls the turnout – and his own servant, so he would not be much trouble and might prove a pleasant companion.

I don't know how we shall like it to have our home life invaded by him, but it will be impossible for him to stay at the bungalow, for the compound is dug up preparatory to making the new lawn and it is too unhealthy for anyone to live there during the rains in this age-old country. We can give him the Blue Room for his study and the guest-room with the big four-poster mahogany bed. Did I ever tell you that this bed was brought to India in the time of the East India Company? Things which came out in the old days are passed on from one to another. A friend said when she first called that she admired a certain chair and decided to buy it when I left India.

To continue, R can have the dressing-room, bath, and east verandah, so he can be very comfortable. He can write at night to his heart's content when a story takes possession of him and 'the child must be born'. These Indian bathrooms are very different from ours at home. The floor is of hard *chunam* (plaster), with a high partition for the tub, which is filled as needed by the *bhisti*[10] from his goat-skin, which is suspended from his shoulder. The Blue Room has every convenience and is quite private, with its own verandah and entrance from the hall. Kadir Baksh can take complete charge of his master and his part of the house. His man is quite a character. He is tall and commanding in appearance and is wholly dependable, which is well, as Rudyard, who lives in the clouds, needs some earthly care.

July. The Pioneer publishes a weekly paper containing stories, poems, and sketches, a kind of supplement called *The Week's News*, for which the youthful editor was expected to write a story filling several columns. His first notification of this was in seeing, as he came from the north into Allahabad, a huge advertisement in the railway stations saying that 'Rudyard Kipling, author of *Plain Tales from the Hills*, will write a series of stories for *The Week's News* beginning with the next number.' This did not disturb the young man, whose only difficulty was in getting time from his routine work to write out the tales with which his brain was teeming. There was no extra payment for these stories.

Allahabad, July. Dear J: When 'The Man who Would Be King'[11] was germinating in RK's mind he was lunching with us. Suddenly he demanded names for his characters. A promptly said, 'Well, the queerest name I ever heard was that of a missionary I met in the Himalayas when we were both tramping – "Peachey Taliaferro Wilson".' Of course Rudyard seized that at once. I could think of no name to give, so R said, 'Well, who was the most prominent man in your home town?' Of course you know that I replied 'Mr Dravo,' and sure enough he used these very names, adding a *t* to Dravo.

Later he was sitting at a desk busily writing. A was in a big chair and I was near by. His custom was to push off a sheet from the pad as fast as he had filled it with his tiny fine writing, letting it fall to the floor. A picked up the sheets, read and passed them to me, our one complaint being that we could read this thrilling story faster than the author furnished it.

Speaking of 'His Majesty the King,' RK said he had a very tender corner in his heart for little children, but there was not often an opportunity for showing it.

I never saw anyone more devoted to children, and alas there are so few in this station; all old enough have been sent to England, but Dr and Mrs J. Murray Irwin have a darling little girl who is my godchild. When she comes to the house there is nothing that R will not do to amuse her. He plays bear, crawling over the floor, and he will endure every sort of teasing. On her birthday he wrote to accompany my small gift a gay little verse beginning,

> Imperious wool-booted sage,
> Tho' your years as men reckon are three,
> You are wiser than ten times your age
> And your faithfullest servants are we.

At last RK is coming into his own, for he is permitted to collect the stories he has written for *The Week's News* into a more permanent form to be published by Wheeler,[12] in the Railway Edition. The covers are to be a greyish blue and the Pater is designing them.

The first one, of *Soldiers Three*, came for inspection and has been severely criticised by Ruddy. Mulvaney is not smart enough in the way he stands, and the barracks are not just right. I shall keep the pencil sketch, as it will be interesting to compare.

What a life he leads, all among the babblings of the Chamber of Commerce and the unsavoury detail of the days among the dockets, departmental orders, and the queer expositions of human frailty, vanity, greed, and malice that a newspaper offers. With it all he watches for suggestive ideas for his tales. For instance: –

'The Judgement of Dungara'[13] had its origin in a statement that A made at the dinner table concerning the Nilgiri nettle, which has most persistent stinging qualities. R made use of every item of information he could gain, and in a few days the story of the great God Dungara appeared in *The Week's News*. It has a vivid description of the loneliness of a mission station in the interior. 'Isolation that weights upon the waking eyelids and drives you by force head-long into the labours of the day.' The missionary, besides giving his flock the Bread of Life, had taught them to weave white cloth from the glossy fibres of a plant that grew near by. The Civil Service official was due, and the converts, usually naked, were to appear for the first time clothed in their new garments, made, alas, from this terrible nettle. It was woven fire that ran through their limbs and gnawed into their bones. Needless to say, they broke ranks and rushed to the river, 'writhing, stamping, twisting and shedding garments pursued by the thunder of the trumpet of the God Dungara.'

The need in India for hospitals for native women is very great. Dr Bielby,[14] the Kiplings' physician at Lahore, was going home to England, so she was asked to present to Queen Victoria the dire necessity for some help for the secluded zenana women.[15] She did so, and as a result the Lady Dufferin Fund for a chain of hospitals throughout India was raised by means of everyone giving a day's pay, from the richest rajah down to the humblest ryot – from the Viceroy to Tommy Atkins. This stirred the soul of Rudyard, so he wrote for *The Pioneer* 'The Song of the Women'[16] – prefacing the poem with the address of the women of Uttarpara to Lady Dufferin which had been published in *The Pioneer*. 'Our feelings in this matter are shared by thousands of our sisters throughout the land and of this we are assured by many signs not likely to come under the observation of the outside world.'

Kipling brought the first copy of the paper just fresh from the press to us and, tossing it over, said, 'What do you think of that?' He is rather cynical about the whole matter, for the giving of money is not voluntary, but practically compulsory.

Kipling's friends felt that it was unfair to him to keep writing stories for the two papers without any extra renumeration, so he was persuaded to discontinue them. He wound up with 'The Last of the Stories'.[17] He pictures a visit of his old friend, the Devil of Discontent, who lives at the bottom of the inkpot, but emerges half a day after each story has been printed with a host of useless suggestions for its betterment. This Devil of Discontent is the proprietor of the largest hell in existence, the Limbo of Lost Endeavour, where the souls of all the characters go. He takes the author below, where his characters are passed in review before him – till his heart turns sick. 'The Last of the Stories' closes, 'Now the proof that this is absolutely true lies in the fact that there will be no other to follow it', and there were no more for *The Week's News* – a great loss to the Indian public. He was not permitted to sign any of his work.

We invited Rud to stay at our house while we are away, as he is at the NWP[18] Club and he could have more room and also enjoy Bhoj's cooking. He has written of his good times and of his trials.

It seems that the ayah thought this was her opportunity for a tamasha, so she celebrated by having guests in the compound. That meant noisy ekkas[19] jingling down the avenue and the night, vocal with much tinkling of anklets to the accompaniment of the sitar.[20] Rud says he had no notion that forty poor rupees could create such a devilment for so long.

Evidently he is not idling, as he says Mulvaney 'came' with a rush on the blue couch in the Blue Room, and if he walked one mile up and down as he was hacking it out, he walked three. Old 'Pig and Whistle' is getting lame, so R is pattering about in the dust, to his infinite weariness and discontent.

September. Dear Ones: You know we live in a famous old bungalow which has been standing since the Mutiny days of 1857, when nearly every house was destroyed. RK so appreciated the privilege of staying in our lovely home while we were away that he wrote a clever sketch for us which tells of our daily life, our occupations, and our servants. He pictures the attractive verandah where we live most of the time, the long avenue of thick-leaved shisham trees leading to the house, and he gives many amusing incidents. He calls this 'Celebrities at Home', borrowing the title from a series of articles now coming out in an English paper.

Some day maybe I'll send you the manuscript, which is at first in his fine handwriting, but toward the last is hurriedly scribbled.

December. *The Week's News* demanded a Christmas story which would fill a whole sheet of the paper. RK brooded over this awhile; the result was 'Baa, Baa, Black Sheep', which is a true story of his early life when he was sent with his little sister to England to be educated. It is next to impossible to bring up English children in India, not because they could not have literary advantages here, but on account of the bad influence the close contact with the native servant has on the child. He is a slave to every whim, so Sonny Baba grows too domineering to suit the fancy of an English parent. No self-reliance can be learned while under the pampering care of bearer or ayah. Also, once a *chi chi* accent – as English contaminated by a native tongue is termed – is acquired, it is rarely lost even after years of later life in England, and pure speech is an essential, according to an Englishman. 'Baa, Baa, Black Sheep' recounts Kipling's experiences at the hands of Aunty Rosa, the stern Englishwoman who made her living by taking in the little waifs from Anglo-India who must be separated from their parents. The hardest choice a woman must make in India is to decide whether it is best to go home with her children or stay with her husband.

A friend took Ruddy and Trix from Bombay on the long sea voyage, and saw them established in the 'home', where little Trix was adored and petted but Ruddy was accused of story-telling. There was great jealousy of his brightness in contrast to that of the son of Aunty Rosa. He learned to escape punishment by deceit, and there was no one to teach him the difference between right and wrong. He, poor child, at six was left in the house with a servant while Trix was taken off on a holiday with the mother and her son. Ruddy read and read from the boxful of books that his father had sent him, reading from daylight to dark, till he had devoured them all; then, forlorn indeed, having strained his eyes and being utterly alone, he entertained himself by measuring the whole house hand over hand.

It was pitiful to see Kipling living over the experience, pouring out his soul in the story, as the drab life was worse than he could possibly describe it. His eyesight was permanently impaired, and, as he had heretofore only known love and tenderness, his faith in people was sorely tried. When he was writing this he was a sorry guest, as he was in a towering rage at the recollection of those days. His summing up in the closing words shows the influence on his whole life.

We are just as much Mother's as if we had never gone. Not altogether, for when young lives have drunk deep of the bitter waters of hate, suspicion, and despair, all the love in the world will not wholly take away that knowledge, although it may turn darkened eyes for a while to the light and teach faith where no faith was.

Rudyard was planning to go direct to England, when suddenly the idea occurred to him that he would like to see something of the world first, and as he had helped us look up routes he begged to be allowed to accompany us. Then Mr Allen asked him to write letters on the trip for the *Pi*, which would pay his expenses. We agreed to have him join us, so he writes that he will arrive 'an awful grimy dirty unshaven bricklayer and the great —— will perchance come down to the station and blandly tumble over me and then go home and tell his friends that my journey is solely undertaken in the interests of *The Pioneer* and I shall loaf down the platform with an unclean pipe in my mouth and then I'll be fairly embarked on the way to the high seas.'

Calcutta, 9 March 1889. Here we are, ready to start on our long journey to climes unknown. Rud has loaded us up with a delightful array of books, and he proudly exhibits two black leather manifold books in which he plans to write his 'Sea to Sea' letters for *The Pioneer* with an occasional 'turnover' for the *Civil and Military Gazette* of Lahore, his first love.

He has just received *Wee Willie Winkie*, with its attractive cover designed by his father. This is the inscription for my presentation copy:

> I cannot write, I cannot think,
> I only eat and sleep and drink.
> They say I was an author once,
> I know I am a happy dunce,
> Who snores along the deck and waits
> To catch the rattle of the plates,
> Who drowns ambition in a sea of Lager and of Tivoli.
> I cannot write, I cannot sing,
> I long to hear the meal bell ring;
> I cannot sing, I cannot write
> I am a walking Appetite.
> But you insist and I obey –
> Here goes!
>   On Steamer *Madura*,
> Now rolling through a tepid sea,
> March 10th
>   to Mrs Hill from me,
> A journalist unkempt and inky
> With all regards, *Wee Willie Winkie*.

The covers were torn off from the whole six of the Wheeler edition on account of some postal law, and the letterpress sent on to England to Andrew Lang, so that Ruddy may be already introduced when he arrives in London.

The Babu at the Meteorological office at Allahabad will collect the 'Sea to Sea' letters as they appear in *The Pioneer* and bind them, so we can have a record of our trip without keeping a diary, though all India will be looking on.

16 March. I was present at the inception of Ruddy's *Barrack-Room Ballads.*[21] We were on the British India steamer *Africa* sailing toward Singapore, standing by the rail, when he suddenly began to hum, 'Rum-ti-tum-tra-la' – shaking the ashes from his pipe overboard. I was used to this, knowing something was stirring in his brain. Humming in a musical tone, he exclaimed, 'I have it. I'll write some Tommy Atkins Ballads', and this idea kept simmering for months, with an occasional outbreak in soldierlike language. While we were at Moulmein lunching by a graceful pagoda hung with tinkling brass ornaments at the slender top and with a very broad base, he put forth the opinion that the Burmans had simply copied nature in their building, pointing to a nearby toddy-palm tree,[22] and certainly the shape was identical, while the tinkling resembled the rustling of the leaves.

Yokohama, Japan, 11 May. We are sailing today for America. When Ruddy went to the shop to buy books for our Pacific trip he found an American pirated edition of his own tales. He was so furious that he stalked out of the shop and bought us nothing, to our great dismay. He declared that he would pronounce a curse on the American people in his very next letter, and for one thing it should be on the slovenly way in which Americans speak – just like servants – for the English are so particular about pure speech. I think it is because their lower classes drop the '*H*' or use dialect, as we do not. When R met a girl on the steamer who spoke with a very Southern accent he said his curse was working, though we noticed that he was very devoted to this same sweet maiden from South Carolina.

Beaver, Pennsylvania, July. Mr Kipling has arrived after his Western tour, where he had many experiences, novel and trying. He seems very happy to be once more with his Anglo-Indian friends, for he has been lonely without letters from his home people. He is settled in the rooms at the College, where he has a living-room with open fireplace, a spacious bedroom and bath. There is a couch, where I think he spends most of his time, smoking, reading, and meditating, but not doing much writing. He is absorbing the experiences which are so different in Pennsylvania surroundings from his Lahore days.

A has a dark room rigged up at the College and the negatives made on that wonderful trip are being transformed into memory-books for Rudyard, ourselves, and others.

Beaver, August. I've been painting a set of dessert plates with a design of our wild flowers to take back to India. One day Mr Kipling, who has seemed unusually preoccupied, demanded china and paint. We wondered what project was being evolved in that fertile brain and now we know, for he has put upon six fruit plates some clever verses, about ten lines each, which he painted directly on the china without any notes.

His subjects are Plums, Peach, Berries, Water-melon, Apples, Grapes.

I'll copy the verses soon. They are rather badly painted in dark blue, as he was not accustomed to china paints and did not know how to use the turpentine. We tried to help, but he was too speedy for us.

The time has arrived for another parting, as A's leave is nearly up. RK will meet us in New York, to sail with us on the *City of Berlin*. We shall leave him in London to achieve his worldwide fame, as he is sure to do. In his visits to Washington, Philadelphia, Buffalo, and Boston he has made many friends; he has gained new material for his writing, and he feels that his American experiences have been well worth while. He behaved quite decently while at Beaver, for when he felt grumpy he kept it to himself. The servants were puzzled by him, especially when he demanded that the barber shave him in bed. He swapped stories with our Senator and townfolk, arousing interest wherever he went.

Now we are off for our five years of exile.

NOTES

1. One of the leading teaching universities in India; built in the Saracenic style.
2. Scottish scholar and writer (1844–1912), well liked, with wide-ranging interests (e.g. fairy-tales and medieval French metres).
3. First printed in *Lippincott's Monthly Magazine*, Aug 1890; collected in *Mine Own People* (1891).
4. First printed in *Week's News*, 28 Apr 1888; collected in *Black and White* (Allahabad: A. H. Wheeler, 1888).

5. Intimate conversation.

6. An off-print paper of *The Pioneer,* using already-published materials, but with its own editorials.

7. A collection of eight stories and one poem (Allahabad: A. H. Wheeler, 1888).

8. A town in the Dehra Dun district of the United Provinces, on a ridge of one of the lower Himalayan ranges. Today in the state of Uttar Pradesh, India.

9. A collection of seven stories published in New York (1896), and in England under the slightly different title *Soldier Tales* (1896).

10. Water-carrier, especially of a household or a regiment.

11. Collected in *The Phantom 'Rickshaw and Other Stories* (Allahabad: A. H. Wheeler, 1888).

12. See above p. 60, n.1.

13. First printed in *Week's News*, 28 July 1888, under the title 'The Peculiar Embarrassment of Justice Krenk'; collected in *In Black and White*.

14. Elizabeth Bielby was the author of *The Use of Antipyrine in Chest Diseases of Childhood* (1885).

15. Women in an East Indian harem who live in a secluded house.

16. First printed in *The Pioneer*, 17 Apr 1888, and added to the fourth edition (first English edition) of *Departmental Ditties and Other Verses* (1890).

17. First printed in *Week's News*, 15 Sep 1888; collected in *Abaft the Funnel* (1909).

18. North-west Provinces.

19. Light, two-wheeled, one-horse, one-passenger carriage used in India.

20. Musical instrument popular in India. A member of the lute family, with a large body, long neck, and a varying number of strings.

21. The first English edition of *Barrack-Room Ballads and Other Verses* was printed in 1892, and contained the same poems as the American edition that appeared in the same year under the different title *Ballads and Barrack-Room Ballads*. Four poems were added to the second American edition, and three of these four appeared in *The Seven Seas* (1896). In 1899 *Ballads and Barrack-Room Ballads* and *Departmental Ditties and Other Verses* were combined, and published in the Trade and Swastika editions by Doubleday and McClure. Later American editions have used the combined form. (It has been said that the history of Kipling's bibliography is the most complex of any modern author).

22. The palmyra-palm yields a fresh sap that can be fermented and used in a hot drink, consisting of an alcoholic liquor, water, sugar and spices (often garnished with fruit).

Opium in India – a Medical Interview with Rudyard Kipling*

ROBERT H. M. DAWBARN

A few years ago it was the writer's privilege to spend a part of an evening chatting with Mr Kipling, at the Authors' Club, in New York City. More exactly, Mr Kipling did the talking, and I, with a thirst for information from the land of Mulvaney and the memsahib, aided and abetted by plying him with questions. Among other topics touched upon was the opium habit as found among the natives of India.

Naturally, from the author of 'The Gate of a Hundred Sorrows',[1] I expected a scathing denunciation of the drug, and of those whose cupidity, in high Government positions, invites its general usage. Instead, Kipling spoke of it as the friend, and in certain ways the mainstay, of millions there among the natives. He said that there is an admitted difference between races in their reaction to its habitual use. A native takes it increasingly up to a certain point, and does not then as a rule go beyond this for the rest of his life – just as is the case among white men with tobacco, at least for a great majority of its users. But the white *habitué* of opium generally does not stop. He steadily increases his dosage until a wrecked life is the result.

Kipling claimed as an indisputable fact that in India the native regular eaters of opium are strengthened thereby for arduous labours; and more important and striking as a statement, he asserted that these men are comparatively free from 'the fever of the country' – a severe and prostrating form of malaria, common among the rice paddy-fields, the many hundreds of square miles of low, swampy land swarming with a native population. He also said

* *Therapeutic Gazette* (Detroit), XVI (15 Nov 1900) 721–3.

that opium is effective in treating this fever. . . .

Continuing, he remarked that he had often been exasperated at the 'mote-and-beam conduct' of English clergymen regarding opium. They go out to India during a brief vacation, for example, and will of course see there an occasional instance of opium intoxication; though, Mr Kipling claimed, such are rather infrequent. Even so, this poor sinner is never violent, harming no one but himself; and being soporose, or even semicomatose, when well under the narcotic, never attacking others.

Then such clergymen, returned to their English churches, will preach rancorously against the opium traffic in India – its evils having been witnessed by themselves; meanwhile deliberately overlooking the crying home evil of drunken and quarrelsome men, women and children upon the streets of every English town.

All of which, be it observed, is Kipling's statement, not mine.

I inquired as to the prevalence in India of the hashish habit, which is said to hold in various parts of the world as many, or more, millions in thrall than does opium. Kipling asserted that but little *Cannabis indica* in any of its forms is used in India; and that little mainly among the Mohammedans and the well-to-do. It is considerably more expensive in India than is opium, he says; which fact would of itself account in great measure for the difference in popularity among a people so miserably poor.

He concluded with a quite poetical description of the white poppy-fields, enormous in extent, and gleaming with a silvery sheen in the moonlight. In Bengal alone a quarter-century ago there were more than a half million acres devoted to the production of this drug. This number is greatly increased now.

Kipling described the regular method of collecting the opium. Immediately after the fall of the flower the natives in great numbers, each armed with a peculiar knife so arranged as to cut, quite lightly, each poppy-head thrice at a stroke, rush through the poppy-fields in the early dusk, working as long as they can see; or else doing it just before sunrise. The jelly-like juice that exudes from the cuts is scraped off, as a rule, at daybreak twenty-four hours later.

This jelly is subsequently placed in vessels 'where it is beaten and at the same time *moistened with saliva*' (US Dispensatory). Pleasing thought! One which should at least go far to prevent, if not to cure, the opium habit!

NOTE

Dr Dawbarn was Professor of Surgery at New York Polyclinic Medical School and
Surgeon to the City Hospital, New York.
    1. First printed in the *Civil and Military Gazette*, 26 Sep 1884, and collected in
Plain Tales from the Hills (1888).

'Bumptious and Above his Station'*

GEORGE SEAVER

Whilst Younghusband was engaged with his work on the Staff of the
QMG,[1] newspaper reporters would flock to the office for
information. Among them was a very dark young man with bushy
eyebrows, large spectacles, and unhealthy appearance, named
Rudyard Kipling, in search of copy for the *Civil and Military Gazette*
of Lahore. 'He was looked upon with great disfavour by Staff
officers as being bumptious and above his station.' When in later
years Younghusband came to recognise him for what he was, a
supreme literary genius and a poet of Empire, he said that he
admired the manner rather than the matter of his work, both in
prose and verse.

NOTE

George Fenn Seaver (b. 1890) wrote three books on Edward Wilson, naturalist and
friend, and books on Nicolas Berdyaev and Scott of the Antarctic.
    1. Quarter Master-General.

* *Francis Younghusband: Explorer and Mystic* (London: John Murray, 1951)
pp. 36–8.

Part IV
Success in England

The Earliest of the 'Plain Tales'*

MAX PEMBERTON

My introduction to Kipling and his genius was curious.

One day there stalked into the office of *Vanity Fair*, then the leading society journal, a tall and stern ex-Jesuit who had quitted the order for the very good reason that he had to go out into the world to support his sister.

Speaking with unwanted earnestness, he declared that he had discovered a genius, and he proceeded to throw down upon the table a little book bound in green paper covers and emanating from India. It was a volume containing some of the earliest of the 'Plain Tales from the Hills'.

How much I wish that I had seized upon that trifle: today its market value is, I suppose, somewhere about a thousand pounds.

A month or two after this, all literary London was talking Kipling, the younger people especially stressing the ballads. Well do I remember the astonishment of the great Mudford,[1] the famous Editor of the old *Standard*, when his nephew quoted at his dinner table the well-known lines 'Oh! the 'oont, Oh! the 'oont, Oh the gawd-forsaken 'oont!'[2] The old gentlemen could not make head or tail of it, but he thought it very shocking.

Shortly afterwards I was set a difficult task by certain estimable people who had invited that great American writer, George Cable,[3] to come to London. 'You must give a dinner to Cable at the Reform Club,' they said, 'and you must get Kipling.'

My answer was that they might as well expect me to get the Emperor of China and his mother. They, however, persisted, so I sat down at last and sent Kipling a wily telegram. He, at that time, declined flatly to go even to quasi-public dinners and 'receptions'

* *Kipling Journal*, VII (Dec 1939) 38–9.

were abhorrent to him. None the less I tried it on.

'Cable is here,' I wired, 'America would take it as a great compliment if you were present at the dinner about to be given to him at the Reform.'

Well, he fell for it – and Tree, who heard of the business, was so good as to declare that I was the 'best social diplomat in Town'.

Not very long after this Kipling was having a few merry encounters with his American publishers, Doubleday and Page. They objected to his title, 'A Day's Work',[4] for one of his novels. He cabled back: 'Why not "a Doubleday's work"'?

The same years saw him in a pretty mood when the Editor of *Appleton's Magazine* quarrelled with his bias toward alcohol. 'One of your sea captains', the editor cabled, 'drinks a glass of hot rum when he is at sea. Could not you substitute a non-alcoholic beverage?'

In reply Kipling cabled, 'Why not try Mellin's Food?'

NOTES

Max Pemberton (1863–1950) wrote a large number of romantic novels and revues and plays. He edited *Chums* (1892–3), and later *Cassell's Magazine* (1896–1906). Founder of the London School of Journalism (1920), he rose to become Director of Northcliffe Newspapers.

1. William Heseltine Mudford was the second son of William Mudford, famous author, journalist, and Editor of the *Courier* in the first half of the nineteenth century; he himself edited and managed the *Standard* up to 1900.

2. Part of the refrain of 'Oonts (Northern India Transport Train)'. First published in the *Scots Observer*, 22 Mar 1890; collected in *Departmental Ditties, Barrack-Room Ballads and Other Verses* (1890).

3. Cable (1844–1925) was a well-known novelist who took New Orleans as his special theme. See *The Grandissimes* (1880), *Madame Delphine* (1881) and *Bonaventure* (1888).

4. Twelve stories published under the title *The Day's Work* in 1898, in both England and the United States.

Some Kipling Memories*

On 20 January 1936, a few days after Kipling's death, *The Statesman*, an Indian paper with a very wide circulation on the sub-continent published a long article made up mainly of recollections by an anonymous writer who obviously had known him well. It is too long and rambling to reprint in full, but some anecdotes do not seem to have appeared elsewhere and are worth quoting.

About *Plain Tales* we learn that as the first edition 'was small and running out of print rapidly, a second edition was issued, the history of which is curious. The publishers thought with good reason that it might do well in England; so, with this idea they shipped a thousand copies to London in sheets to be bound and published in the metropolis. This small issue was the foundation of Kipling's fame. At the time, he was scarcely known at all outside of India. The only person of any note who had noticed him was Andrew Lang; and it was in part owing to a personal letter from him that Kipling decided to launch his craft in the old country.

'The London office of Thacker, Spink and Co.[1] had the greatest difficulty in finding a market for the thousand copies of *Plain Tales*. In this case a prophet was certainly without honour. No one would look at it. But – and this is another story – the *Saturday Review* had its attention drawn to the book and published a very fine review, which at once opened out the market.[2] Kipling arrived in England to find himself on the borders of fame. And it is curious that one of the first letters he opened on his arrival was a note from India to say that the account of his travels published there was a failure! This series was afterwards published [as] *From Sea to Sea. . . .*'[3]

The Light that Failed was issued as a special supplement to *Lippincott's*. This last was written under peculiar circumstances. A representative of *Lippincott's* approached him with the offer, but it was coupled with the proviso that the manuscript should be delivered in a week. It was assumed, of course, that he had a long

* Unsigned article in *Kipling Journal*, XL (June 1973) 4–5.

story ready for delivery. Kipling had always been in doubt whether he could last over the 'long course'. He had nothing at all to suit at the time, but he accepted the offer and also the stipulation. Then he worked day and night, finishing the book in four days from receiving the commission. The effort was more than he could stand and he was seriously ill in consequence. There is another phase to this episode and that is how he came into possession of the plot. But that is a sacred confidence. . . .

'It is natural that Kipling should have possessed the eccentricities of genius. In his chambers [in Villiers Street][4] he had a huge roll-top desk at which he did his work. He probably picked it up second hand. He also had a Gurkha kukri,[5] a particularly fine one with a razor edge. With this same kukri he carved on his desk in letters at least six inches high 'Oft was I weary when I sat at thee.'[6] When he was thinking out details of a story, he would sit in a chair and chop at the sides with his kukri, reducing his furniture to fragments.

'Kipling's unpublished stories of his experiences in America were often rather priceless. He landed in San Francisco an unknown man. But of course the ubiquitous interviewer got on his track. To Kipling's original mind this was a beautiful opportunity for a "scoop" and before the luckless young man could get back to the paper with his story, Kipling had weighed in with an interview with the interviewer, which so charmed the Editor that the interviewer's own manuscript had a back seat. . . .

'A man of strong personality, his conversation bristled with aphorisms. "No man can write until he has loved and suffered." "A good writer absorbs experiences as he goes through the world and spews them out as an owl does the remnants of his food, the hair and bones of the rodents he has assimilated. . . ." Kipling had a poor idea of his own powers as a poet. His contention was that poetry was a useful medium for expressing forceful ideas where they could not be so expressed in prose. His method as he told the writer many times was to get a tune in his head and fit words to it. . . .

'He loved Sir Henry Irving,[7] and although he could have had seats for the asking, always preferred to crowd into the pit, where he would wait for an hour or more so as to get a front seat. There was a distinct method in this madness, as he gained much character study from his entourage on such occasions.

'Kipling was not a person who attracted at first sight. But the charm of the man was irresistible when one got to know him. His brilliant talk, his intense family love, and enthusiasm over what he considered right; and, moreover, his curious capacity for making the acquaintance of interesting people. There was the outstanding case of the amiable giant of Babbacombe.[8] But that again is another story!'

The author of this article is not named, but an account of his interview with W. H. Pollock, too long to quote here, proves that it was by C. F. Hooper[9] who was working in the London branch of Thacker Spink and Co., in 1889, and who tells the same story almost verbatim in a signed article in the *Saturday Review* of 7 March 1936.

NOTES

1. The Calcutta publishing-firm purchased *Departmental Ditties* from Kipling for 500 rupees, and later published *Plain Tales from the Hills*. Copies of the latter sold well in India, but the 1000 copies sent to England took several years to find their market.

2. 'This review, which appeared on 9 June 1888, was by the Editor, W. H. Pollock. See *Kipling: The Critical Heritage* (1971) p. 36' (note by Editor of *Kipling Journal*). Walter Herries Pollock (1850–1926) edited the *Saturday Review* (1883–94); wrote lectures on French poets, and graceful essays on fencing, animals, and acting, as well as a number of books of poems. His most notable essay in criticism is *Jane Austen: Her Contemporaries and Herself* (1899).

3. Two volumes of letters, sketches, and stories written before 1900. The first American edition appeared in 1899, and the first English edition in 1900.

4. Kipling lived here, off the Strand, between 1889 and 1891. The building in which he stayed is today called the Kipling House.

5. The Gurkhas used a curved knife, a 'kukri', broader at the point than at the handle. Its keen edge is usually on the concave side.

6. In Kipling's short story 'The Finest Story in the World', Charlie Mears, who remembers his life as a galley-slave in an earlier incarnation, records his handcuff-scratchings in 'extremely corrupt Greek' on an oar. These, in turn, are translated by an expert at the British Museum as meaning 'I have been – many times – overcome with weariness in this particular employment.' (Kipling is paraphrasing a line in Longfellow's 'The Broken Oar'.)

7. The first actor on whom knighthood was conferred, Sir Henry Irving lived from 1838 to 1905.

8. Babba's valley near Torquay, Devon, gives its name to the bay. The giant (probably a real person rather than a figure from folklore) is unidentified.

9. Hooper, a member of the firm of Thacker, Spink and Co. shortly before Kipling left India, persuaded the Editor of the *Saturday Review* to print a review of *Plain Tales from the Hills*. It helped to establish Kipling's name in England.

Kipling's First Appearance*

DESMOND CHAPMAN-HUSTON

Apart from his manifold services to literature and journalism, if Low had never done anything but encourage Kipling in the early struggles of his English career, he would have deserved well of mankind. There are certain phases of the life and civilisation of our times portrayed by Kipling that will be accepted by posterity as bearing the hall-mark of the highest authenticity.

Low never claimed to have 'discovered' Kipling, though he had a better right to do so than many of the numberless people who like to pretend that they were the literary godfathers of the great. Low was, however, without any question the first person to print an original article by Kipling in any English periodical: the story, which has its modest place in the history of literature must therefore be told in his own words:

It was in the late autumn of 1889, when I had succeeded Frederick Greenwood[1] as Editor of the old *St James's Gazette*, then a famous London evening journal with a high literary reputation.

Kipling had just returned from India after his seven years' service (which he began as a boy of seventeen) with the Lahore *Civil and Military Gazette*. In India he was already known by those short stories sold at the railway bookstalls in thin paper-covered volumes, which are now worth a good deal more than their weight in gold. Some of these booklets, and the *Departmental Ditties* had come into my hands through Stephen Wheeler, once Kipling's editor at Lahore, and then a valued member of the *St James's* staff.

My interest and curiosity were aroused at once. I spent an afternoon reading *Soldiers Three* and when I went out to a dinner-

---

* *The Lost Historian: A Memoir of Sir Sidney Low* (London: John Murray, 1936) pp. 78–83.

party that evening I could talk of nothing but this marvellous youth who had dawned upon the Eastern horizon. My host, a well-known journalist and critic of those days, laughed at my enthusiasm which he said would hardly be justified by the appearance of another Dickens. 'It may be', I answered hotly, 'that a greater than Dickens is here.'

I got Wheeler to put me in touch with Kipling on his arrival in London, and one morning there walked into my office a short, dark, young man, with a bowler hat, a rather shabby tweed overcoat, an emphatic voice, a charming smile, and behind his spectacles a pair of the brightest eyes I had ever seen. He told me that he had his way to make in English literature, and intended to do it, though at the time he was young, very poor, and (in this country) quite unknown. I suggested that he might help to keep his pot boiling by writing sketches and short stories for the *St James's*, which suggestion he willingly accepted. He also accepted my proposal to come out and lunch with me.

We sat down in the grill-room of Sweeting's Restaurant in Fleet Street.[2] I wanted to 'draw' Kipling, and I drew him to some purpose by getting him to tell me about places he had seen in India and elsewhere. He was in no wise reluctant, being exceedingly frank and communicative, and overflowing with ideas and memories which had to find vent; and he talked in those days with the same abandon and energy as he wrote.

One after another of the lunchers laid down knife and fork to listen to him, and presently he had half the room for his audience. He was quite unconscious of the attention he evoked, as he remained long after his face had become familiar to all the world.

A day or two later he sent me a contribution, which I received with delight and promptly printed. This, so far as I know, was the first piece from Kipling's pen published in England.

It was a miniature story in his best 'early manner', full of drama, incident, and atmosphere, and all compressed into some 1500 words. I always thought it a pity that Kipling never republished this little thing, and left it in the anonymous obscurity of a now-forgotten journal.

Its author sent me several more sketches and stories during the next few months, when he was working feverishly in a humble lodging off the Strand, writing for many hours of every day and night. His sojourn in Grub Street was, however, brief. I knew, of course, that I should not be able to keep him long; this fresh, vivid, and striking talent was bound to gain speedy recognition.

I did try to attach him regularly to my staff by the offer of as liberal a contract as the limited resources and circulation of the paper would permit. Kipling declined the proposal in a long letter of doggerel verse. He said he had put off the journalistic harness after his seven years of it in India, and did not care to be fettered by it again. Shortly afterwards he published 'Without Benefit of Clergy'[3] and 'Greenhow Hill'[4] with half a dozen other of his best tales in *Macmillan's Magazine*,[5] and then the *Barrack-Room Ballads*, and jumped at once into unbounded popularity. Editors and publishers were tumbling over one another to get copy from him, and he could ask his own terms for a story or a poem.

He found time, however, in those busy years in his early success, when he was so rapidly becoming one of the most celebrated and sought-after of living authors, to do something occasionally for the *St James's*.

He always liked 'The Jimmy' as he called it, and was quite disproportionately grateful for the little help I was able to give him at the outset of his English literary career. So from time to time he would drop in on me with an article, or a copy of verses, usually suggested by something he had seen in the paper. One such occasion came in 1891, when the *St James's Gazette* had opened a fund for the relief of the survivors of the Balaclava Charge.[6] This drew Tennyson, who sent me some fine verses in support of the appeal; and Tennyson's lines drew Kipling, who wrote his 'Last of the Light Brigade'[7] as a sequel or commentary.

The efforts of the Elder and the Younger Master resulted in a substantial sum being placed in my hands for distribution, and an immense amount of trouble afterwards in sifting the applications of ancient soldiers, most of whom were very clearly 'not the Six Hundred'.

Kipling declined to take any payment for his poem. He also sent a donation of £5 to the Relief Fund with the request that I should lump it under the subscriptions of the *St James's Gazette* office.

Low is, of course, referring to the *St James's* when he says,

We had been writing strongly in support of a bill, then before Parliament, intended to prevent unscrupulous ship-owners from risking the lives of sailors by sending ships to sea in a dangerous condition.

One morning Kipling strode into my office and began at once with breezy vehemence, 'I say, you know, I like those screeds[8] of yours on the coffin-ships. Do you want a poem about them?'

I assured him I did.

'All right', he replied; 'give me some paper, something to smoke, and something to drink, and you shall have it.'

I supplied his simple needs, put him a room by himself, and left him in what the novelists of the period would have called 'the throes of composition'. They were easy throes for Rudyard Kipling *anno aetat.* 26.

In about half an hour, or a little more, I went in to see how he was getting on. 'Here's your poem', he said. 'Would you care to hear it?' And then, in his rich, sonorous voice, he rolled out the resounding lines:

Seven men from all the world back to Docks again,
Rolling down the Ratcliffe Road, drunk and raising Cain.
Give the girls another treat 'fore we sign away;
We that brought the *Bolivar* out across the Bay![9]

And so on for twelve stanzas. That was the first time 'The Ballad of the Bolivar' ever fell upon human ear. I wonder how many thousands of ears have been thrilled (and occasionally tortured) by its subsequent recitation?

Kipling handed me the copy of the poem. It was written, in his exquisite neat and tiny handwriting, on one side of a single sheet of paper, without a correction or erasure. I sent the MS. to the printers, with instructions that it was not to be cut or in any way defaced, and returned to me.

It is noteworthy that when Kipling in due course revised the *Ballad* only one word was altered by the poet: in the line 'Yoke the kicking tiller-head' the last word was changed to 'rudder-head'.

By mid-April 1895, Kipling was back in England from a prolonged visit to America and he and Low met almost at once and had 'much talk about the States'; this was soon followed by another long talk 'concerning strikes and other things', and Low asked for some American impressions. According to Low's diary Kipling said, 'every nation was proud of what they hadn't got: Americans of their law-abiding character, English of their domestic virtues, Germans of their literature'. However, Kipling was tired writing about America, and some criticisms of Low's regarding *Barrack-Room Ballads* led to a humorous threat to take in the *Pall Mall*. The United States at the time was seething with strikes and Low did in the end manage to wheedle out of Kipling an article on the subject. It was accompanied by a characteristic note. Dated only one week later than the talk, it illustrated the author's punctuality in keeping his promises, than which nothing is more pleasing to editors and publishers.

NOTES

Major Desmond Chapman-Huston (Wellesley William Desmond Mountjoy, 1884–1952), born in Ireland, led an active life as politician, soldier, essayist, and biographer. He edited *Subjects of the Day*, by the Marquess Curzon of Kedleston, KG. His book on Sir Sidney Low (1857–1932) deals with a crucial episode during Low's editorship of the *St James's Gazette* (1888–97).

1. English journalist and man of letters (1830–1909), Editor of *Cornhill Magazine* and *Pall Mall Gazette*, and novelist (*Margaret Denzil's History*, 1864).

2. No. 70 Fleet Street.

3. First published in *Harper's Weekly*, June 1890; collected in *The Courting of Dinah Shadd and Other Stories* (1890).

4. The story 'On Greenhow Hill' first appeared in *Macmillan's Magazine* in September 1890, and *Harper's Weekly* in August 1890; it was collected in *The Courting of Dinah Shadd and Other Stories*.

5. Also published in this periodical were 'The Courting of Dinah Shadd' (Mar 1890), 'The Man Who Was' (Apr 1890), and 'The Incarnation of Krishna Mulvaney' (Dec 1890).

6. The battle took place on 25 October 1854, near Balaclava, a village in south-western Crimea. A charge by some 600 men of the Light Brigade was immortalised in Tennyson's 'The Charge of the Light Brigade'.

7. First printed in the *St James's Gazette*, 28 Apr 1890; first authorised book-edition, 1908; first printed in Kipling's collected volumes in *Verse, Inclusive Edition* (1919).

8. Long, tiresome harangues (especially lists of grievances) or letters.

9. 'Ballad of the *Bolivar*', first published in the *St James's Gazette*, 25 Mar 1890; collected in *Barrack-Room Ballads and Other Verses* (1892).

Kipling among the Early Critics*

E. W. MARTINDELL

In 1898 Dr Kellner, author of the *History of English Literature in the Victorian Era*,[1] described in the *Neues Wiener Tageblatt* a visit he paid to Kipling at Rottingdean. He summed up his impressions in the phrase, 'Today I have seen happiness face to face.' This is what he said about his visit: 'The workroom is of surprising simplicity, the north wall is covered with books half its height, over the door hangs a portrait of Burne-Jones, to the right, near the window, stands a plain table on which lie a couple of pages containing verses. No works of art, no conveniences, no knick-knacks, the unadorned room simple and earnest like a Puritan chapel. "I do my daily task conscientiously, but not all that I write is printed: most of it goes there." The waste-paper basket here received a vigorous kick and a mass of torn-up papers rolled on the ground. The Puritanic strain in his nature came out the more strongly at the moment when others – like Burns, for example – have lost their hold on themselves in the hour of triumph. Kipling is never so distrustful and self-critical as when he has around him the cries of praise. "I am very distrustful against praise," said he, "very distrustful against fame. You know the fate of eighteenth-century English literature, how many 'immortal poets' that prolific time brought forth, and yet how much of this 'immortal' poetry still lives in our time? To name only one, who reads Pope nowadays? I often run over these volumes here" (here he pointed to the Edition de Luxe of his works, published by Macmillan) "and think to myself how much of that which is printed on such beautiful paper ought never to have seen the light. How much was written for the love of gain, how often has the knee been bowed 'in the House of Rimmon'?"[2] (a favourite expression of

---

* *Kipling Journal*, VIII (Apr 1941) 9–11.

Kipling). All that fate – Kipling would call it "the good God" – has to bestow of real worth has been granted to this wonderful child of fortune; love, domesticity, independence, fame, and power in the vigour of his youth (he is only thirty-two) and sound health, and above all, the capacity for enjoying his good fortune. Nor is that all; Kipling has the happiest fortune which can happen to a man when he has attained his highest aims, his father and mother are still alive, and he can and does say with proudest modesty, "All that I am I owe to them." "The annexation of one white nation by another," he said, "I regard as the greatest crime that a politican can commit. Don't annex white men." "How about the blacks?" "I am against slavery," was the answer, "if only for this reason, that the white man becomes demoralised by slavery." He is an ardent admirer of Cecil Rhodes, whom he knows personally and whose work he is able to judge from his recent visit to Matabeleland. "How did you get on with Rhodes? What sort of a man does he appear?" was the question to which the answer came: "Rhodes is greater than his work . . . "

He interests himself in all literary work of the day, and is at home in all the chief movements and side currents in the spiritual life of England. When discussing the *Literary History of England* [which Dr Kellner has in hand] Mr Kipling said, "If I had your book to write I would attempt in a final chapter to discover the path which may lead from the present chaotic conditions of our literature and that of the twentieth century. I would call the chapter 'Between Two Epochs'. I feel that we are between ebb and flood. It is now just what sailors call 'slack tide'; we are waiting for the great personality which will unite all the minor tendencies of the time and collect all the partial and petty forces into one power that will give a new and adequate expression to the new time." Dr Kellner concludes his remarks with the question, 'Is that man still to come, or is he already here?'

NOTES

E. W. Martindell (1866–1933) compiled *A Bibliography of the Works of Rudyard Kipling (1881–1923)*, which appeared in 1922, and *The English and Empire Digest*, which summarised every English case reported from early times to the present day (i.e. 1919, and brought up to date in 1930).

1. Leon Kellner wrote *Die englische Literatur im Zeitalter der Königin Viktoria* (Leipzig, 1909).

2. Ramman, called Rimmon (2 Kings 5:18) in the Old Testament. The Assyro-Babylonian god of thunder and storms; also a war-god, sometimes depicted with a hammer.

The House of Macmillan (1843–1943)*

CHARLES MORGAN

Kipling's letters to the firm are even fewer and less illuminating than Henry James's, and that for a particular reason. Three of the earliest settle a small point of bibliography. One speaks of the *Plain Tales'* successor by what was at that time its title: *The Book of the Forty-Five Mornings*;[1] the others prove that this was not, as has been authoritatively supposed, the first name of *From Sea to Sea* but of *Life's Handicap*.[2] Soon afterwards, when Craik made an inquiry of Kipling about continental rights, the reply came from A. P. Watt,[3] the agent, and thenceforward everything from Kipling was at third hand – through Mrs Kipling, through Watt. Kipling was more suspicious of publishers than Byron himself, but had not the grand manner which enabled Byron's affability towards Murray. Byron thought of them as tradesmen and knew how to treat tradesmen; Kipling had a different point of view and would never have been at ease, even in Albemarle Street.[4] Part of his prejudice may have dated back to his experience with *Departmental Ditties*, turned out on the office plant of the *Civil and Military Gazette* and sold by the sending out of reply-postcards. Thus all middlemen and sinners had been eliminated. 'There was', as Kipling said, 'no trade discount, no reckoning of twelves as thirteens, no commission, and no credit of any kind whatsoever. The money . . . was transferred from the publisher, that left-hand pocket, direct to the author, the right-hand pocket.' The effect upon his mind of this profitable if primitive experience was reinforced by less fortunate experiences in America, where his earliest work was ruthlessly pirated before it could receive the benefit of the 1891 Act. Not only did he receive no payment, but, much worse, material he had wished to suppress was reprinted, and

* (New York: Macmillan, 1944) pp. 150–2.

he was driven in self-defence to publish it in *Abaft the Funnel*,[5] which was not allowed to appear in England until released for the Sussex Edition.

Therefore Kipling, as author, fenced himself in, though Kipling, as man, was on the best of terms with his publishers when he met them privately. Macmillan's kept his prose and Methuen's his verse, except *Songs from Books*.[6] It became, as the years passed, almost a game to invent new dresses for his work – uniform editions, pocket editions, the Edition de Luxe in red and gold, the Bombay Edition, the Service Edition intended for the pack or pocket of soldiers in the 1914 War. There were, also, school editions, and gigantic volumes in which all the dog stories or all the Mowgli stories or all the humorous stories were assembled, and year by year the wise men held their breath and wondered whether by now the public demand for old wine in new bottles was exhausted. The cautious feared it might be, but they were always wrong. It may be hoped that Kipling gave his publishers credit for an inventiveness in the use of a selling-machine more elaborate than his reply-postcards. Certainly he knew his own value, and Macmillan's, even if they had wished to do so, had not the power to reduce the price of his books. But the luck was bound to turn, and it turned with the most costly, complete and ill-fated of all his 'limiteds' – the red-leather Sussex Edition. Of this there were thirty-five volumes in 500 sets. Special hand-made paper was used, great care was given in St Martin's[7] Street to every detail of production, and Kipling, playing his part with unfailing courage, wrestled with ill-health so that he might add to it material excluded from other editions and revise his whole work. Before it had begun to appear, he died. The edition proceeded, but the demand was less than had been looked for, and fate decreed that the Sussex Edition should not be allowed to wait for a new generation of collectors. The unsold sets and unbound sheets were stored with the binders in Kirby Street, EC.[8] An air-raid buried them, and before many could be disinterred the building was struck again, and all but a few odd volumes were destroyed. When visitors in St Martin's Street are given a chair newly upholstered in red leather, it is upon what would have been the binding of the Sussex Kipling that they sit.

NOTES

Charles Langbridge Morgan (1894–1958) succeeded A. B. Walkley as the principal drama critic of *The Times* (1926). His novels – *The Gunroom* (1919), *My*

Name Is Legion (1925), *Portrait in a Mirror* (1929), *The Fountain* (1932) and *The Voyage* (1940) – were well-regarded by both critics and the public. His essays were collected in two volumes in *Reflections in a Mirror* (1944–6). He took pride in the fact that he and Kipling were the only English-born members of the Institute of France.

1. In 1891 Kipling intended to publish some letters, but abandoned the project. It is probable that *From Sea to Sea* (1899), a collection of letters, sketches, and stories, replaced his original concept.

2. First English and American editions, 1891.

3. Alexander Pollock Watt, the Scottish intermediary between authors and publishers and editors, believed that he invented the concept of the literary agent.

4. On this street are located both the publishing house of John Murray and Brown's Hotel, Kipling's favourite stopping-place in London.

5. A series of stories published in 1909. Kipling first used the title for eight stories written for the *Civil and Military Gazette*.

6. A collection of poems published in 1912.

7. Home of Macmillan before it moved to Little Essex Street.

8. In Hatton Garden, EC 1, the home of jewellers, artists, photographers, etc.

Authors and I*

C. LEWIS HIND

In 1889 we in London who were living by literary journalism, began to talk with awe and wonder about a new Anglo-Indian author called Rudyard Kipling, whom his intimates addressed as Ruddy.

My friend Vernon Blackburn[1] got to know him and to idolise him; and it was through Vernon that I began to hear wonder talk about Rudyard Kipling. He was not a society man, or a frequenter of clubs: he was a worker, an investigator of London humanity, like O. Henry in New York, a prowler about the streets who would copy the names of striking thoroughfares in his notebook, and talk to anybody who was engaged on an interesting job. He was an old young man, who checked and chided Vernon's youthfulness. Sometimes Vernon would be admitted into the Kipling workshop. He told me how the author of *Barrack-Room Ballads* would rush to the window when a soldier passed down the street; how he would

* (New York and London: John Lane, 1921) pp. 166–170.

compose stanzas at white heat, one after the other, and rush upstairs each time to read the new effort to his parents; and how once when he was declaiming 'The Blind Bug' to Vernon, and had reached the line 'He flipped the blind bug into the dark' he suited the action to the word so vehemently that the blood spurted.

We bought, not without difficulty, and read and reread those collections of stories, in blue paper covers, with the imprint of an Indian publisher – *Soldiers Three*,[2] *In Black and White*,[3] *Under the Deodars*[4] and all the other wonders of prose and verse. For a poet, too, a writer of swinging, haunting verses, who used slang without fear and without reproach, was this young Anglo-Indian who took young literary England by storm.

The dons of Oxford and Cambridge were rather shy of Kipling, but the undergraduates opened their Norfolk jackets to him, and by 1890, when he published *Life's Handicap*,[5] and in 1891, *The Light that Failed*, he had won his way almost into the ranks of the 'best-sellers'. *Barrack-Room Ballads* was not published till 1892 and by that time even the Quarterly Reviewers were almost ready to accept his violent wayfaring with the tongue that Shakespeare spake. Of course when *Kim* was published Kipling became a classic.

W. E. Henley had prepared the way for the introduction of *Barrack-Room Ballads* into the fortresses of classicism by publishing them week by week in the *Scots Observer*. Henley, being joint author with Farmer of the *Slang Dictionary*,[6] was of course vastly interested in Kiplingese. Reading the proofs in the office of the *Scots Observer* in Westminster, he would roar with laughter and hammer the table with blows of delight. One of the ballads especially pleased him. Turning to me he said, 'Will you take this telegram when you go?' He handed it to me. It contained three words: 'God bless you!'

Parties and functions are not for Kipling. He is no hermit, but his friends have to be of his own choosing. I heard about the oyster supper parties he gave when he was living in one of the dim little streets by the Thames near Charing Cross, and once I was taken by Vernon Blackburn to see him in the house that his father had rented in the Earl's Court Road. It was a Saturday afternoon: he was at work before a roll-top desk, and carved upon it (he did it with his penknife) were the words, 'Oft was I weary when I toiled at thee.' He read us the poem he was then writing. No, he did not write it out: his mouth was his pen. That has always been his way, to compose a poem in his head, to get it right and taut, and when it is all done to copy it out on paper in his clear, small handwriting. He read fiercely.

The next time I saw Rudyard Kipling was under rather shameful circumstances for which I was not responsible. I was staying at Rottingdean, a seaside place in Sussex,[7] and, having an idle hour, succumbed to the blandishments of a *charabanc* conductor to see the sights of the neighbourhood. We were driven past the village-green and pond, past the Burne-Jones dwelling to a white house in a garden surrounded by a high wall. 'Sight No. 1', shouted the conductor. 'This is the house of the celebrated author, Rudyard Kipling.' The conductor craned his neck, rose on his toes, and said, in an excited voice, 'If you will stand up, ladies and gentlemen, you will see the celebrated author in a garden hat, just entering his porch.' Can you wonder that soon afterward Mr Kipling moved from Rottingdean and settled in a delightful old house near Burwash, in Sussex, where there are no *charabancs* and no tourists?

Once more I saw him – a chance encounter. I was cycling from Rottingdean to London, and in a puncture interval at a wayside blacksmith's encountered him in a mess of grease and rags assisting in taking a motor-cycle to pieces. That was the mechanical Kipling, the author of the difficult-to-read mechanical, technical stories.

There was nothing technical, just sheer inspiration, in the article that appeared in the London *Spectator* describing how Shakespeare, strolling one afternoon into the pit of the Bankside Theatre, fell into coversation with some sailors, plaited hair and rings in their ears, and obtained from them the seafaring knowledge that he used in *The Tempest*. The article was unsigned. We wondered who the author might be; we sought in vain. Years later an American publisher issued this article as a pamphlet-de-luxe. It was signed Rudyard Kipling.

And there was nothing technical about the speech he made at a Royal Academy banquet, one of his rare appearances in public, wherein he gave an account of the first artist, he who took a charred stick from the fire and made a sketch on a rock of his companions bringing home a deer. 'How did it go?' I asked a Royal Academician. 'Great!' he answered. 'Great! We were spellbound.'

NOTES

C. Lewis Hind (1862–1927) wrote dozens of books on artists, such as Turner, Augustus Saint Gaudens, and Aubrey Beardsley, and published numerous treatises on landscape-painting. He edited *Art Journal* (1887–92), *Pall Mall Budget* (1893–5) and *The Academy* (1896–1903).

1. Musical critic of the *Pall Mall Gazette*; worked for *The Tablet and the National Observer*.

2. Publication No. 1 in the Indian Railway Library, containing seven stories and one poem (1888); first edition in England, 1890.

3. Publication No. 3 in the Indian Railway Library; first edition in England, 1890.

4. Published in Allahabad by A. H. Wheeler, 1888. Most of the contents had previously been published in *Week's News*.

5. First American and English editions, 1891.

6. John Stephen Farmer (1845–1915), co-editor with W. E. Henley of *Slang and Its Analogues Past and Present* (first printed 1890).

7. A sea-bathing resort close to Brighton, Sussex, on its eastern side.

Kipling's First Story*

IAN HAMILTON

Looking back over a long life I feel grateful indeed to God for having so wonderfully answered the prayer of a small boy for a good wife. Time after time I taxed Jean's patience but her patience and understanding were always forthcoming in full measure and truly only once – once to the best of my belief – was she really hurt by my behaviour. I had written a small volume of verses and had as usual handed them over to her for her advice and remarks. At that time I was in constant touch with Rudyard Kipling. Every Sunday I lunched with him at the house of Lord 'Hatband' Russell (afterwards Duke of Bedford)¹ together with Walter Lawrence,² and one way or another hardly a day passed when I did not see him. He knew about these verses and was keen that his sister Trix, a charming girl and favourite dancing partner of mine – nothing more – should take a look at them before she went back to England. Jean was out so I nipped the manuscript off her table and sent it to

* *Listening for the Drums* (London: Faber & Faber, 1944) pp. 201–4.

Trix for perusal and return. That's all!! Only a storm in a tea-cup *you* may say, but, speaking as a husband, *I* say give me a storm on the ocean.

Fifty-five years later there has arisen a curious sequel to this Ancient Mariner yarn. On 17 August 1942 I was dining with some literary friends one of whom told us Kipling never took money for a poem as an instinct warned him that if he did he would never write another. Several of the company at table disputed this statement either because they thought they had proofs of the contrary or for some other reason. The argument waxed high and promised to be inconclusive, so I chipped in saying I would write to his sister Trix and she could probably would authoritatively settle the question. Here is her answer:

4 West Coates, *Edinburgh* 12

20 August 1942

My dear Sir Ian,

What a pleasure to hear from you again. I purposely held back from writing to you when the Parting of the Ways came, though my thoughts and prayers were constantly with you both. . . .

To the best of my belief and recollection, it was only poems of a serious sort that Ruddy took no money for. See p. 148, ch. 6 of *Something of Myself* – about 'Recessional' – 'I gave it to *The Times*. I say "gave" because for this kind of work I do not take payment. . . . I should not like the people whose good opinion I valued to believe that I took money for verses on Joseph Chamberlain,[3] Rhodes, Lord Milner,[4] or any of my South African verse in *The Times*.'

All his life long he drew a careful distinction between verse and poems. In one of our last talks together he said he could only lay claim to having written a dozen poems in the whole of his life – 'No, too many – half a dozen more likely. The rest were just verses.' Some of those verses were, I believe, paid for in three figures. His two literary agents – his wife the first and keenest – a true business Yankee, and Mr Watt kept a firm check upon his generous impulses.

He told me – by word of mouth – that before the launch of the *Queen Mary* he was offered a blank cheque for appropriate verses and replied, 'Let Masefield[5] do his own job, he used to be a sailor.' He certainly had very strong feelings about his Daemon and the possibility of a gift used unworthily being withdrawn. In my lesser degree I had the same feeling in my fortune-telling days – unless every penny went to charity I knew I should 'lose my faculty' – though I sometimes gave offence by declining a new fancy dress – White Witch – or Sibyl – 'out of the funds'. A reputable Greek insurance firm in Calcutta once offered me a handsome salary ('no deductions for failures but a good percentage for successes') if I would occasionally read the hands of applicants for insurance!! I was not tempted . . .

Yours ever,
Trix Fleming

Many people seem to think that Kipling suffered none of those rebuffs and disappointments which fall to the lot of most young authors. The truth was otherwise. As I was the means of sending his first story to England, the following anecdote as to its adventures may be of interest.

In 1886 I wrote to Vereker,[6] who was then in London, telling him I had been seeing a good deal of a young fellow called Rudyard Kipling, who had a pretty talent for writing and was anxious to publish something in England. I told him that the manuscript of a short story selected by the author would soon reach him and suggested that he might show it to Andrew Lang, the author of *Ballads in Blue China*,[7] and William Sharp who wrote as a woman under the *nom de plume* of Fiona Macleod,[8] with both of whom he was well acquainted and then to the editors of two magazines, after which he was to report the results.

Kipling's manuscript duly reached V and was sent off to Lang. It was soon returned under cover of a very strong letter of condemnation one sentence of which is firmly imprinted on my memory: 'I would gladly give Ian a fiver if he had never been the means of my reading this poisonous stuff which has left an extremely disagreeable impression on my mind.' Lang went so far as to say that any attempt to make a start in English literary circles with a magazine article of this nature would be most detrimental to the author's chances of future success supposing, even, he could get anyone to touch it which he very much doubted. It is only fair to add that some years later Lang changed his view of Kipling as a writer and extolled his work with both voice and pen.

Lang's verdict was so uncompromising that V thought the chances that Sharp would think favourably of the manuscript were greatly increased; for it would have been difficult to find two men more different in their tastes and points of view. He therefore sent the story to Sharp with some confidence that it would appeal to him. William Sharp's reply was even more decisive – indeed quite extraordinarily so. William Sharp said, or at least this was the gist of his remarks, 'I would strongly recommend your brother's friend instantly to burn this detestable piece of work. If I would not be considered to be going beyond my brief' (here I really do remember the actual words), 'I would like to hazard a guess that the writer of the article in question is very young and that he will die mad before he has reached the age of thirty.'

The manuscript continued its travels. It visited in turn the editors of the two magazines but these gentlemen very quickly sent it back, V began to be nettled. At first, he wrote me, he had been only mildly interested in the adventures of the manuscript, but the rebuffs which had been flung at what appeared to be a strong and original little story, irritated, and also puzzled him. So he decided to have a try-out on his own.

'I decided, before returning the manuscript to India, to read it out to a selected audience of young painters just to see what impression it would make on them', he wrote in his book *Things that Happened*. 'My audience consisted of my wife, two or three other ladies and my old fellow students, Holroyd,[9] Furse,[10] and Strang.[11] Their names were unknown to the general public then, but in course of time each of them made his mark – Sir Charles Holroyd as Director of the National Gallery; Charles Furse as a brilliant painter; and William Strang as an etcher. Strang indeed was a mass of energy who worked with equal thoroughness on copper, paper, canvas or wood. They all possessed liveliness of imagination and independence of view, so they were a good audience for such a test as I proposed.

'The reading took place one night in my studio and the outcome was that the story was greeted with enthusiastic appreciation by the whole company. It was agreed that there was a strong flavour of the horrible in the tale; but our literary taste was not thin-skinned and this flavour did not prevent the company from admiring the originality of the theme and the style in which it was narrated. The manuscript then went back to India.

'For a few years nothing more was heard of it; and then, suddenly it appeared again in England – this time in the full light of publicity for Kipling had meanwhile made his name. It formed one of several short stories in a volume which had an instant success. The original story had not been altered in any particular but it had been given a new title – "The Mark of the Beast".'[12]

At this period I got two goes of leave home in very short succession; the first time Kipling being absolutely unknown: the second time 'Rudyard Kipling' being words to conjure with as I realised at a grand dinner party at Arthur Balfour's[13] at Whittinghame consisting mainly of literary celebrities, 'Souls' and people of that sort. Sitting there a shy and unconsidered guest it became known that I had associated with Rudyard Kipling in the flesh. Instantly the grand people there assembled were silenced by Lady Frances Balfour,[14] in order that they might all share in the excitement of listening to one who had actually met the hero of the hour *in propria persona*.

NOTES

Sir Ian Standish Monteith Hamilton (1853–1947) served in Ireland (1872–3), and in India for twenty-five years, where he improved the musketry efficiency of his troops. Aide-de-camp to Sir Frederick Roberts, then Commander-in-Chief, Madras. A record of valour in South Africa and elsewhere. He opposed compulsory service, and clashed with Roberts (before World War I). Later, he led the doomed Dardanelles Expedition. Author of *A Staff Officer's Scrap Books* (2 vols, 1905–7) and *Gallipoli Diary* (2 vols, 1920), among other books.

1. Arthur Herbrand Russell, 11th Duke of Bedford (1858–1940), in the Grenadier Guards in the Egyptian campaign (1882); aide-de-camp to the Viceroy of India, Lord Dufferin (1884–8); succeeded his elder brother as Duke of Bedford (1893). In 1888 he married the daugher of Walter Harry Tribe, Archdeacon of Lahore.

2. Sir Walter Roper Lawrence (1857–1940) entered the Indian Civil Service in 1877; served as Under-secretary to the Punjab Government (1884–6) and to the Government of India (1887–9); was officiating secretary to the Government of India (1889), and private secretary to Lord Curzon of Kedleston, Viceroy of India (1899–1903).

3. Joseph Chamberlain (1836–1914), statesman and politician, strengthened British dominions in Australia and Africa; served as British Colonial Secretary (1895); and played a controversial role in the Jameson Raid. The breakdown of his negotiations with the Boers led to the outbreak of war.

4. Alfred Milner (1854–1925) governed Cape Colony (1897–1901), and was High Commissioner for British South Africa (1897–1905).

5. John Masefield (1878–1967), English poet, dramatist, novelist, and poet

laureate from 1930 on. Famous for 'Sea Fever' and 'Cargoes', among many other works.

6. Vereker Monteith Hamilton (1856–1931) wrote *Scenes in Ceylon*, and provided both the text and illustrations for *Things that Happened* (1925). He was brother to General Ian Hamilton.

7. Published in two volumes in 1890–1.

8. Scottish poet, critic and editor (1855–1905); an important figure during the Irish Literary Renaissance (1880–1920). Wrote under the pseudonym of Fiona Macleod, supposedly a Highland poetess and his cousin. The secret of his true authorship was not revealed until after his death.

9. English painter and etcher (1861–1917), noted for his landscapes and views of Venice.

10. Charles Wellington Furse (1868–1904) was a pupil of Alphonse Legros at the Slade School, London, and a member of the Julian atelier in Paris. He became famous for his portraits of distinguished figures (e.g. Lord Charles Beresford), oils of horses, and paintings in Liverpool's Town Hall. He assimilated artistic influences of Whistler, Sargent and the Japanese.

11. Scottish painter, etcher, book-illustrator and print-maker (1859–1921). His portraits of authors are particularly notable.

12. First published in *The Pioneer*, 14 July 1890, and collected in *Life's Handicap* (1891).

13. Arthur James Balfour, 1st Earl of Balfour (1848–1930), led the House of Commons as a Conservative (1891–2, 1895–1900, 1900–6) and as Prime Minister until the Liberal landslide of 1906. He succeeded Winston Churchill as First Lord of the Admiralty, and was the chief British delegate (1921–2) to the disarmament conference at Washington, D.C. The Balfour Declaration favoured limited Jewish settlements in Palestine.

14. Church-woman, ardent suffragist, and author (1858–1931). Daughter of the 8th Duke of Argyll; married (1879) E. J. A. Balfour, brother of Arthur Balfour. Organised the rebuilding of Crown Court Church, London.

A Story of Rudyard Kipling*

ARTHUR REED KIMBALL

One evening, so Kipling's friend relates, Edmund Yates[1] sat down to dinner at his club, wondering what would make a good, stirring article for his paper – the London *World*. He asked a friend at an adjoining table if he did not know of something that was going on.

* *The Independent (New York)*, XLIV (7 Apr 1892) 473.

Replied the friend, 'Why on earth don't you print an interview with Rudyard Kipling?'

'Who in thunder is Rudyard Kipling?' asked Yates.

The friend, who was acquainted with India and with Kipling's career there, explained that he was a very brilliant young fellow, who knew India as few men know it, for he had a remarkable faculty of observation; that he had just come home, bringing with him a volume of stories which he had published; that he must have with him, also, a large stock of interesting memorabilia; that in his (the friend's) opinion Kipling was the coming man in story-telling; that it would be greatly to the credit of Yates's paper to anticipate the public in discovering him; that he would at any rate have much to say that was fresh and interesting.

The idea struck Mr Yates as a good one, and he detailed one of his reporters immediately to interview Kipling. The reporter had some difficulty in finding Kipling, for his lodgings were obscure, and his disgusted publishers had not kept close track of his address. But found he was at last, and, when found, he had all the hauteur of confident genius when most prosperous in being on the whole rather unwilling to submit to the un-English advertisement of an interview. The reporter prevailed upon him to do the favour (Kipling's friend said that he understood as well as any one the help the publicity would be to him, and was simply playing a game of bluff). So the interview appeared, some two columns in a much-read paper. It created no little talk. Among others who read it with interest was the book-reviewer of the London *Times*. He remembered, in an indistinct way, that Kipling's stories had come to his desk, and that he had let them lie there. He hunted them up, and in the light of what he now knew about the man, was greatly impressed by them. He gave them a half-column review or more, and that with a great many Englishmen was enough. To find Kipling endorsed in *The Times* immediately set them to reading him. The stories no longer lay, dust-covered, on the publisher's shelves. The stock on hand was not sufficient to meet the sudden demand.

How long it would have been before the world discovered Kipling, had not Edmund Yates asked a friend, whom he met at dinner in his club, for some subject for an article, may be left to those who care to speculate on the unknowable. For the rest of us it is sufficient that Kipling was found out, and a fresh story-teller of genius added to the world of literature which seems to so many to be so nearly exhausted in its constant readaptions of the same old plots in changed situations, and of the same old characters under different aliases.

Speaking of Kipling, with whom the friend for a time shared apartments, he said that Kipling's methods were strictly reportorial, after a literalness that would delight Howells. For example, their rooms were just off the Thames Embankment, near the Waterloo Bridge. This is a quarter frequented at night by many of the rough-and-ready characters which have figured in some of Kipling's later stories. Of a summer evening Kipling would draw his lounge up to the window, leaving the window open, and lie there, pencil in hand, listening, jotting down any of the coarse repartee that seemed to him unusually funny, or the racy talk that seemed to him typical of the class. He thus gathered not a little material, which he worked literally into his pages.

NOTE

Kimball (1855–1933) wrote *The Blue Ribbon: What Thomas Edward Murphy has done for the promotion of personal temperance, with some account of the work of his father, Francis Murphy, and of his brother, William J. Murphy* (1894), and an article on 'Yale as a University at the Threshold of the Third Century' (*The Outlook*, 5 Aug 1899).

1. English journalist and novelist (1831–94), Yates wrote a column on 'personalities' from 1855 onward for the *Illustrated Times*; he also wrote about society for *The World*. His controversial critiques of Thackeray, Lord Lonsdale, and others, made him a somewhat notorious figure.

Kiplingiana*

Captain E. W. Martindell sends us the following extracts from an interview with Kipling, which Mr Roger Peacock contributed to *Lloyd's Newspaper*, 4 January 1903. Thus Mr Peacock writes:

'I have to tell the story of an interview made for the Press, but held back for several years until it could be sent to men who will understand . . . After I had waited respectfully on the doormat

* *Kipling Journal*, VIII (July 1941) p. 24.

while the maid enquired, Mr Kipling had me let in on approval. Very tame, very meek, I was admitted to a library smelling pretty strongly of tobacco, and in the far side of the room, in a cloud of smoke, a tweed suit, and large spectacles, sat a man like a large bronze idol. "Sit down", said he, and I did. "I'll have my knife into the man who sent you. Where's your pipe?" I lit up, and in a state of panic asked the first question which entered my head. "Who told you the 'Rhyme of the Three Sealers'?"[1] "Mind your own business!" "I've the right to know; had the yarn in my notebook for years before you printed it." "Where did you get it?" "From one of the Yokohama pirates, the Flying Dutchman." "So you knew Hans? Where?" "In Behring Sea." "Then you've the right to know. I got it from Captain Lake in Yokohama. So you're a pirate?" "Yes, and your 'White Seal' contains an idiotic blunder. A fur seal sleeps with his fore flippers folded on his breast, not limp at his sides." "Confound you", he grunted. So I went on asking questions and we fought like cats for ten minutes. Then he leaned forward half-visible in smoke, shining, bronzed, his eyes veiled by the light on his spectacles – Buddha come to life, staring through me, whispering suggestions. I smelt the dust of a trail, heard the creak of the saddle, felt between my knees the heaving flanks of a horse, and the Great Plains reaching away forever, and then his voice dispelled the vision. "Don't you wish you were back?" Again his whispering voice caught me away, and I knelt in a dug-out canoe, hearing the paddles grind along her gunwale, feeling the thrill of her tail as her nose dipped into the ripples. I saw the oily rush, the coiling pools, the lifted waves, the diamond-crested breakers, as we swept into the rapids–"Don't you wish you were back?" Once more the whispers went through me, and I felt the heave of the big ocean swell, the lifting deck under foot . . . "Don't you wish you were back?" I thrust out my hands against him. "Shut up, you devil!" And he grinned like a bronze image. Not only had he been interviewing me, but found out more about me in ten minutes than my parents ever knew. So he interviews everybody, getting each man's facts like a fishwife cleaning a herring before he knows it . . . After I had passed the beak-and-claw department, and come to know the man inside, I began to understand a little the way he came to be great . . . He got his knowledge, not by wasting his time in forecastle, camp, or barrack, not from school, not as the second-hand stuff one gains from printed books. It was learned at first hand from men. His eyes see one through to the bones, his questions are sharp and deep-searching as a surgeon's knife, and his brain files the facts away in a memory as big as a library . . . His questions never give offence to a man of action . . . and his books have been addressed not to idlers or critics, but to workers . . . they are plain, clear reading for the fighters, the workers, the living men of Greater Britain. "You're an Imperialist?" I asked. "I've been suspected", he said, grinning. "The biggest poem you've written so far is the 'Hymn before Action'."[2] "I think so too," he answered, "I got it in church. Think of the hymn tune – 'The Church's One Foundation'."[3] Music runs in his head. Words shape themselves to carry the tune, saying clearly what millions of people have been feeling vaguely. "Tell me", I asked, "why your attempts at novels have failed." "Give a fellow a chance", he answered. "I'm only beginning to grow, and a man can't grow up to writing books under the age of forty. Besides, I don't think the novel is the thing best worth writing." ' Here we come to the end of Mr Peacock's interview.

NOTES

1. First printed in the *Pall Mall Budget*, 14 Dec 1893; collected in *The Seven Seas* (1896).
2. First printed in *The Echo*, Mar 1896; collected in *The Seven Seas*.
3. See above, p. 21, note 2.

'I've Got It All in my Head'*

BRANDER MATTHEWS

I had met Kipling first at the Savile in the summer of 1891 when he had recently returned from India, and when he was in the first flush of his sudden success. At that time it seemed to me that he did not feel quite at home in England; and like most of the men who have

* *These Many Years: Recollections of a New Yorker* (New York: Charles Scribner's Sons, 1917) pp. 432–4.

spent their impressionable years in outlying parts of the Empire, he found it easier to be friendly with an American than with the average inhabitant of the British Isles. I have often observed the fact; I suppose that this immediate fraternising is due to our possession of the same language and of the same traditions, and of our common difficulty in narrowing our vision to the affairs of the little island set in the silver sea. To the American as to the colonial, London may be 'the power-house of the race' – but it is not the whole works. I recall that in 1891 when we were once talking about the insularity of the British, Kipling said, 'Well, I'm not an Englishman, you know; I'm a colonial!' a statement that he would possibly not have repeated a score of years later.

Of all the Englishmen I have ever known Kipling has the most sympathetic understanding of American character. He married an American; he lived for a while in the United States; and his intimate acquaintance with American literature began when he was a boy journalist in India. His friendship is so thorough that he has not hesitated more than once to point out certain of our less desirable characteristics; and this has sometimes exposed him to the charge of unfriendliness. I doubt if we Americans are fonder of flattery or more resentful of candid criticism than the British are or the French or the Germans; and our cuticle is not as tender as it was before the Civil War; but even now we are not as thick-skinned as we might be.

Lovers of poetry are united in holding that its appeal is rather to the ear than to the eye. Even if we must get our knowledge from the printed page, we do not really possess a poem until we have read it aloud and made ourselves conscious of its rhythmical potency. As this is the case, I have been inclined to believe that those lyrics are most likely to please our ears which have been composed more or less completely in the head of the poet, even if they may have been meticulously revised after he had put them on paper. I knew that Scott had beaten out his ballads as he galloped over the hills and that Tennyson had often sung his songs into being while walking in the open air. I was confirmed in this belief when Kipling dropped into my house in New York one day in the nineties and when he answered my query as to what he had been at work on with the information that he had just completed a long ballad. I asked to see it.

'Oh, I can't show it to you now,' he explained, 'for it isn't written down yet. But I've got it all in my head and I'll say it to you if you like.'

When I assured him that this was exactly to my liking, he began to recite 'McAndrew's Hymn',[1] walking up and down as he spoke the vigorous and sonorous lines of that superb story in rhyme, second in Kipling's own verse only to the noble 'Ballad of East and West',[2] and unsurpassed in the work of any other contemporary ballad-writer of our language. The weighty lines and the picturesque movement of the poem lost nothing in the poet's simple delivery. When he had made an end, I cried out my admiration. And then, after my enthusiasm had cooled a little, I hesitated a criticism.

'Are you certain sure that you have all your engineering technicalities just right?' I asked.

'I think so', Kipling replied. 'In fact, I'm almost sure. But I'm going to Washington next week and your chief engineer, Melville, has promised to point out any slips that I may have made.'

NOTES

(James) Brander Matthews (1852–1929) was highly respected in literary and theatrical circles in New York City, London and Paris. He became the first professor of dramatic literature in any American university (Columbia), and exerted a strong influence on playwrights between 1890 and 1915. His major works include *The Development of the Drama* (1903) and *Principles of Playwriting* (1923). *These Many Years* (1917) is his autobiography.

1. First printed in *Scribner's Magazine*, Dec 1894, and collected in *The Seven Seas* (1896).

2. First printed in 1889, and collected in *Barrack-Room Ballads and Other Verses* (1892).

Memorials of Edward Burne-Jones*

LADY GEORGIANA MACDONALD BURNE-JONES

Christmas this year was marked by merriment made for the children in the hall of the Grange – a room whose dimensions I should feel it impious even now to calculate, but it was big enough to shew a magic lantern in and for us to play snap-dragon in, and it seemed very big to the little ones. They had with them their young cousin Rudyard Kipling, now beginning the Anglo-Indian child's experience of separation from his own home, and with our family of two thus increased by one half, we felt there was even more reason than usual for celebrating Christmas Eve. So we gathered together such grown-up friends as were not claimed elsewhere, and who could if needed still romp with a will; Jenny and May Morris[1] brought their parents and Ambrose Poynter[2] his; and they and Edward made for the children a memorable evening. Charles Faulkner[3] and William De Morgan[4] and Allingham[5] enchanted us all by their pranks, in which Morris and Edward Poynter occasionally joined, and Burton's beautiful face beamed on the scene, while Mrs Morris, placed safely out of the way, watched everything from her sofa. This is the last time of the kind that I remember. By the following Christmas the children's own world had begun, and it was their turn to amuse us. . . .

The Little Minister[6] also, which was read aloud to him [Edward Burne-Jones] to beguile convalescence from illness, gave him great pleasure; I shall always remember the way he answered to its beautiful opening and prepared to enjoy himself. Speaking of Mr Barrie before this, he said, 'I like all the books of his I have read; I

* (London: Macmillan, 1906) II, pp. 45–6, 229–30, 312 (article signed 'G B-J').

am glad some one is making tales for me that I shall read with happiness.' When he met the writer, however, the time was not a lucky one; it was an evening of a prepense kind likely to fail, and he regretfully wrote of it, 'I dined out to meet Barrie – Barrie of Thrums. He would not talk at all – but nice and thin and pale to look at. Next morning came Rudyard Kipling, and the contrast was great; so that I gave praise to Allah by reason of his power in diversifying his creatures.' . . .

The arrival of Rudyard Kipling and his family in England in 1896 had been a great pleasure to us. For our own sake we would have liked them to live in London, but that was not the scheme of their life, and they took a house in Devonshire. When, however, they found that climate unsuitable, Edward advised them to try Sussex, and urged their going down to our house at Rottingdean while seeking one for themselves. This was arranged, and at the beginning of June they arrived in the village where, as it proved, they were to remain for the next five years.

The certainty of their bright company always awaiting Edward when he ran down to Rottingdean gave one more charm to the little place. 'O my beloved Ruddy,' he writes, 'I am so glad to be going back to you tomorrow. I am growing tame and like a curate – like an over-anxious curate. So tomorrow to little Rottingdean, to laugh and roar and throw care to the dogs – which is a beast I hate.'

NOTES

The daughter of the Revd George Browne Macdonald (1805–68) and Hannah Jones of Manchester (1809–75), Lady Georgiana (1840–1920) married Sir Edward Burne-Jones (1833–98), and was known to Kipling as his beloved Aunt Georgie. She lived, first, at the Grange, North End Road, Fulham (once the home of the novelist Samuel Richardson), and then at North End House, Rottingdean. She sympathised with the Boers, and occasionally argued with Kipling about politics; but their affection for each other remained true to the end.

1. May Morris (1863–1938) edited the collected works of her father, William Morris, in twenty-four volumes. She was a noted embroidery-designer, editor, lecturer on the arts, and founder and chairman of the Women's Guild of Arts. Jennie Morris, christened Jane Alice (1861), suffered all her life from bad health. See Jack Lindsay's *William Morris, His Life and Work* (London: Constable, 1975), for fuller information on William Morris's relations with his daughters.

2. Famous architect (1796–1886); a founding member of the Royal Institute of British Architects (1834); helped to establish government schools of design; heraldry expert; illustrator.

3. Charles Joseph Faulkner (1834–92) was a member of the firm of Morris, Marshall, Faulkner and Co., manufacturers and decorators. The firm was important in setting standards of taste for modern houses.

4. English novelist, potter, stained-glass designer, and inventor (1939–1917); lifelong friend of Burne-Jones, D. G. Rossetti and William Morris. Author of *Joseph Vance: An Ill-Written Autobiography* (1906).

5. William Allingham (1824–89), Irish poet, author of *Poems* (1850) and *Day and Night Songs* (1855), noted for their national spirit and local colouring.

6. Written by Sir James Mathew Barrie (1860–1937) and published in 1891. The son of a hand-loom weaver of Kirriemuir, Angus, Scotland, Barrie wrote a number of sketches for the *St James's Gazette*, in which Kirriemuir appeared as Thrums. (*A Window in Thrums* was published in 1889.)

'My Friend Rudyard Kipling'*

H. RIDER HAGGARD

I think that the next book I wrote after *Eric*,[1] or at any rate the next that was printed, was *Nada the Lily*,[2] which I began upon 27 June 1889, and finished on 15 January 1890. It is pure Zulu story, and, as I believe I have said, I consider it my best or one of my best books. At any rate, the following letter from my friend Rudyard Kipling seems to show that this story has one claim on the gratitude of the world.

Vermont, USA

20 October 1895

Dear Haggard,

Watt has just forwarded me a letter addressed to *you* from a bee-keeping man who wanted to quote something of a jungle tale of mine. I dare say it didn't amuse you, but it made me chuckle a little and reminded me, incidentally, that the man was nearer the mark than he knew: for it was a chance sentence of yours in *Nada the Lily*

* *The Days of My Life: An Autobiography* (London: Longmans, Green, 1926) II, pp. 16–17, 26–7, 92, 159, 208–9.

that started me off on a track that ended in my writing a lot of wolf stories. You remember in your tale where the wolves leaped up at the feet of a dead man sitting on a rock? Somewhere on that page I got the notion. It's curious how things come back again, isn't it? I meant to tell you when we met; but I don't remember that I ever did.

Yours always sincerely,

Rudyard Kipling

. . . It was about this time that I first made the acquaintance of Mr Rudyard Kipling, who had recently arrived in England, I suppose from India. He was then a young fellow about five-and-twenty, and in appearance and manner very much what he is today. I cannot recall under what circumstances we first met. Perhaps it was at a dinner-party which I gave at my house, 24 Redcliffe Square, to some literary friends. I remember that Kipling arrived late and explained the reason by pointing to a cut upon his temple. Whilst he was driving towards my house his hansom collided with a van in Piccadilly, and there was a smash in which he had a narrow escape. From that time forward we have always liked each other, perhaps because on many, though not on all, matters we find no point of difference. . . .

Now as to the method of romance-writing. It should, in my judgement, be swift, clear, and direct, with as little padding and as few trappings as possible. The story is the thing, and every word in the book should be a brick to build its edifice. Above all, no obscurity should be allowed. Let the characters be definite, even at the cost of a little crudeness, and so with the meaning of each sentence. Tricks of 'style' and dark allusions may please the superior critic; they do not please the average reader, and – though this seems to be a fact that many forget, or only remember to deplore – a book is written that it may be read. The first duty of a story is to keep him who peruses it awake; if he is a tired man and it succeeds in doing this, then, within its limitations, it is a good tale. For instance, when a year or so ago Mr Kipling, who as a rule goes to bed early, told me that he had sat up to I know not what hour and got chilled through reading *The Ghost Kings* because he could not lay it down, it gave me a higher opinion of that work than I could boast before. In romance 'grip' is almost everything. Whatever its faults, if a book has grip, these may be forgiven. . . .

On my return to England I wrote *The Way of the Spirit*,[3] an Anglo-Egyptian book which is dedicated to Kipling, and one that interested him very much. Indeed he and I hunted out the title together in the Bible, as that of 'Renunciation', by which it was first called, did not please him. Or perhaps this had been used before. I was glad to receive many letters from strangers thanking me for it. . . .

Among my pleasantest recollections during the last few years are those of my visits to the Kiplings, and one that they paid me here, during which we discussed everything in heaven above and earth beneath. It is, I think, good for a man of rather solitary habits now and again to have the opportunity of familiar converse with a brilliant and creative mind. Also we do not fidget each other. Thus only last year Kipling informed me that he could work as well when I was sitting in the room as though he were alone, whereas generally the presence of another person while he was writing would drive him almost mad. He added that he supposed the explanation to be that we were both of a trade, and I dare say he is right. I imagine, however, that sympathy has much to do with the matter.

Of late years Kipling has been much attacked, a fate with which I was once most familiar, since at one time or the other it overtakes the majority of those who have met with any measure of literary, or indeed of other success – unless they happen to be Scotchmen, when they are sure of enthusiastic support from their compatriots always and everywhere. The English, it seems to me, lack this clan feeling, and are generally prepared to rend each other to pieces in all walks of life, perhaps because our race is of such mixed origin. In Kipling's case some of these onslaughts are doubtless provoked by his strong party feeling and pronouncements, though the form they take is for the most part criticism of his work. Even on the supposition that this is not always of quite the same quality, such treatment strikes me as ungenerous. No man is continually at his best, and the writer of 'Recessional' and other noble and beautiful things should be spared these scourgings. However, I have no doubt it will all come right in the end, and I hope that when this book is published he may be wearing the Order of Merit.

Nowadays everything is in extremes, and the over-praised of one year are the over-depreciated of the next, since, as much or more than most people, critics, or the papers that employ them, like to be in the fashion. It is fortunate that, however much it may be influenced at the time, the ultimate judgement lies in the mouth of the general public, which, in the issue, is for the most part just. It is fortunate also that only a man's best work will come before this final court, since in our crowded age the rest must soon evaporate.

NOTES

Sir Henry Rider Haggard (1856–1925) was a very popular English novelist; an expert on agriculture; and an acute social critic.

1. *Eric Brighteyes* (1891).
2. Published in 1892.
3. Published in 1906.

'Kipling's Advice to Rider Haggard'*

LILIAS RIDER HAGGARD

The growing strength of his friendship with Kipling was a great joy to Rider. Many of his books went to Rudyard in manuscript for criticism. They planned plots together, discussed their farms and the visits that Rider paid to the Kiplings were the greatest joy and refreshment. . . .

Years later in his book *Something of Myself*, Kipling said much the same of Rider. 'Rider Haggard would visit us from time to time and give us of his ample land-wisdom. His comings were always a joy to

* *The Cloak That I Left: A Biography of the Author Henry Rider Haggard*, KBE (London: Hodder & Stoughton, 1951) pp. 194–5, 259–61, 271–3.

us and the children, who followed him like hounds in the hope of "more South African stories". Never was a better tale-teller, or, to my mind, a man with a more convincing imagination. We found by accident that each could work with ease in the other's company. So he would visit me, and I him, work in hand; and between us we could even hatch out tales together – a most exacting test of sympathy.'

Kipling, who hid so great and sensitive a heart under a brusque and rugged exterior, was not prodigal in his friendships.

Not only were both of a trade but tremendously in sympathy on many points, including Kipling's strong party and imperialistic convictions, for which both men were roundly abused at the time. After Kipling's publication of his 'Recessional', he wrote the following note to Rider:

> Your note did me much good and I thank you for it. I've just come off a fortnight with the Channel Squadron – rather a jolly time. Now any nation save ourselves with such a fleet as we have at present would go out swiftly to trample the guts out of the rest of the world; and the fact that we do not, seems to show that even if we aren't very civilised we're about the one power with a glimmering of civilisation in us. As you say we've always had it somewhere in our composition. But my objection to that hymn is that it may be quoted as an excuse for lying down abjectly at all times and seasons and taking what any other country may think fit to give us. What I wanted to say was – 'Don't gas but be ready to give people snuff' and I only covered the first part of the notion.

This last remark refers to a continuation of the 'Recessional' which Kipling told Rider he wrote but never published. . . .

Rider went down to St Leonards[1] for the winter. Before he came back to Ditchingham[2] in the spring of 1918, he spent a long day with the Kiplings at Bateman's and noticed somewhat sadly how thin and worn Rudyard was looking.

'Seated together in his study while he fiddled about with his fishing tackle with which he tries to catch trout in the brook, we had some interesting hours together. He is one of the two men left living in the world with whom I am in complete sympathy, the rest have gone. . . . What did we talk of? So many things it is difficult to remember them – chiefly they had to do with the fate of man. Rudyard apparently cannot make up his mind about these things. On one point, however, he is perfectly clear. I happened to remark that I thought this world was one of the hells. He replied he did not think – he was certain of it. He went on to show that it had every attribute of hell; doubt, fear, pain, struggle, bereavement, almost irresistible temptations springing from the nature with which we are clothed, physical and mental suffering, etc., ending in the worst fate man can devise for man, Execution! As for the future he is inclined to let the matter drift.

'Like myself he has an active faith in the existence of a personal devil. His humility is very striking. We were talking of our failings, of the sense of utter insufficiency which becomes apparent as one nears the end of one's days, but I commented on the fact that he at any rate had wide fame and was known as "the great Mr Kipling" which would be a consolation to many men. He thrust the idea away with a gesture of disgust. 'What is it worth? – what is it all worth?' he answered. Moreover he went on to show that anything any of us did well was no credit to us; that it came from somewhere else, that we were, in fact, only telephone wires. As for an example he instanced some of our individual successes – 'You did not write *She*,[3] you know,' he said, 'something wrote it through you . . . " He opined in his amusing way that if the present taxation went on much longer he and I would be seen on opposites sides of the Strand selling the "Recessional" and *She* for our daily bread.

'When I left him he told me how delighted he was to have had the opportunity of "a good mental and spiritual clean-out". I think outside his own family there are few – perhaps none – to whom Rudyard opens his heart except myself. With literary people, he remarked, he had little acquaintance and added "But then I don't think I'm really literary, nor are you either!"

'Practically he lacks intimate friends. I remarked that with the exception of himself and one or two others all my friends were gone but I still made acquaintances. "I don't", he remarked grimly. He asked me as I left him exactly how much older I was than himself. I told him ten years. "Then you have the less time left in which to suffer", he replied. He alluded, I think, to a loss which he and I have both suffered – O Absalom my son! my son!"[4] how that cry echoes down the centuries. Poor old boy! John's death has hit him very hard.[5] I pointed out that this love of ours for our lost sons was a case of what is called 'Inordinate affection'[6] in the Prayer Book. "Perhaps," he answered, "but I do not care for ordinate affection – nor do you!" I told him that I did believe that as a result of much spiritual labour there is born in one a knowledge of the nearness and consolation of God. He replied that occasionally this had happened to him also, but the difficulty was to "hold" the mystic sense of this communion – that it passes. Now this I have found very true. Occasionally one sees the Light, one touches the pierced feet, one thinks that the peace which passes understanding is gained – then all is gone again. Rudyard's explanation is that it meant to be so; that God does not mean we should get too near lest we should become unfitted for our work in the world. Perhaps. . . .'

To these years after the war belong the tales *Wisdom's Daughter*,[7] *Heu-Heu, or The Monster*,[8] *The Treasure of the Lake*,[9] *Allan and the Ice-Gods*,[10] and a book called *Belshazzar*[11] which dealt with Egypt and the fall of Babylon.

The plot of *Allan and the Ice-Gods* was worked out one day in February 1922 which he spent with Kipling at Bateman's, their lovely old Tudor house in Sussex. It dealt with the terrible advance of one of the ice ages upon a little handful of the primitive inhabitants of the earth, and in it we meet Allan as a hunter in the days when the world was young. The idea appealed to Kipling and Rider wrote in his diary, 'I never knew a man so full of "light" as Kipling, nor anyone quite so quick at seizing and developing an idea. He has a marvellously fertile mind. We spent a most amusing two hours over the plot and I have brought home the results in several sheets of manuscript written by him and myself.'

Kipling was also much impressed with *Wisdom's Daughter* which Rider read to him in manuscript and at Kipling's request left with him for a more considered opinion. A week or two later he wrote to Rider suggesting revision, much amplification and some softening of the character of She:

The more I went through it the more I was convinced that it represented the whole sum and substance of your convictions along certain lines. That being so, it occurred to me that you might, later on, take the whole book up again for your own personal satisfaction – and go through it from that point of view. I am not suggesting this from the literary side – that is a matter of no importance – but as a means of restating and amplifying your ideas and convictions through the mouth of your chief character. All this on the assumption that I never hid from you, that the whole book is miles and miles above the head of the reader at large. It will not come to its own for a long time, but to those to whom it is a message or a confirmation it will mean more than the rest of your work . . . Damn it man – you have got the whole tragedy of the mystery of life under your hand, why not frame it in a wider setting? (This comes well from a chap who could not write a novel to save himself.)

That's what I suggest for *Wisdom's Daughter* because I know that as you did it, you'd take the woman in hand and through *her* mouth speak more of what is in your heart. You are a whale at parables and allegories and one thing reflecting another. Don't cuss me. You wanted to know what I thought and so I send it you.

To which Rider replied,

As usual you see the truth, which few others do – few indeed. In that book is my philosophy, or rather some of it. The eternal war between the Flesh and the Spirit, the eternal loneliness and search for unity which is only to be found in God, and when wrongly aimed blinds the eyes and seals the soul to light, which (I think) is the real sin unforgivable. In these latter days – thank heaven, I do seem to be grasping the skirts of vision, though they slip from the hand like water. But to describe – to set down! There's the rub! Well, I don't think it can be done with She. But what about the Wandering Jew idea which I think I propounded to you? The direct outrage to the Divinity – the sin incarnate wrought by whom? Pilate's adviser? The resulting separation from the All-surrounding Love and Grace; the slow upward climb through the ages; the fall through the woman, the redemption by way of the woman. Then the periods: Egypt at the beginning of Christianity, the first I suppose. What others? The fight of the Norse Gods against the White Christ for one and then the Crusades. I must think them out. The end in the war. It would take several years – the rest of my life probably. It would be tremendous if only one were given the grace to do it. . . .

To this, Kipling replied,

You aren't choosing any small canvas for your latter years to expiate in, are you, when you turn your mind towards the Jew? Let us be generous while we are about it. The little business might be worked out in a trilogy. Book One would deal with the origin of the man far back. He might be a composite sort of breed, a bit of an Arab, and a bit of a Sephardim; with a Roman ancestor or two in his line. A hell of a school-taught intellectual, who really was no more than politely cruel to the Lord. He did not say in so many words 'Get along with you'; he just hinted to the Figure staggering beneath its Cross that it was blocking *his* way to an appointment. We can guess the appointment; and the whore comes in later too. Or, he might have told one of the soldiers to shove the malefactor out of his light; which the just-minded Latin refused to do – and here is a point, had his reward in later incarnations!

Anyhow you would have to close the First Book with the Crucifixion, but you might do it from the wholly disinterested point of view of the Jew upon whom the Doom has not begun to work. What *he* noticed was the dust-storm that darkened the city, and again interfered with his appointment on the day of the execution, and the row that two or three low-class women made over the fellow's tomb. Book Two leaves one with the whole choice of either the Fall of the Roman Empire or the complete history of the Middle Ages, introduced by a little talk or two between the Jew, and a wandering disputatious little chap of the name of Paul, who seems to have built up some sort of sect upon the words of this Hebrew ruffian of thirty or forty years back. The Jew himself is elderly now and (still ignorant of his lot) looks to be gathered to his fathers before the times get any worse. (He is a *good* Jew remember.) Paul thinks otherwise but won't give his reasons. The Jew attends a Christian service at the very dawn of the Creed, and warns Paul that he has brought his new faith to a market where it will be bought up by the vested interests attached to the service of the Old Gods. Paul doesn't see. From that point you can go on. Dead easy, isn't it?

So the letter goes on. Kipling's vivid and merciless imagination painting in a few swift words scene after scene – the Crusades – the Black Death – the Inquisition – the painfully acquired wealth of the Wandering Jew which when attained worked only fresh horrors and new wars, and he ends,

Now you won't do one little bit of this, but it will help stir you up to block out the first rough scenario, in the intervals of answering demands of idle idiots and helpless imbeciles to which cheerful task I am now about to address myself for the next hour.

Ever thine, R K

Kipling was right – it was not done – the time grew too short.

NOTES

Lilias Ridẹr Haggard was the youngest daughter of H. Rider Haggard. She edited *I Walked by Night: Being the Life and History of the King of the Norfolk Poachers* (1935) and George Baldry's *The Rabbit Skin Cap* (1939). In addition to this biography of her father, she has written *A Norfolk Notebook* (1946) and *A Country Scrap-Book* (1950).

1. St Leonard's-on-Sea, a large suburb on the west side of Hastings, Sussex. Haggard lived there at North Lodge.

2. Haggard's home, Ditchingham House, was located in this south Norfolk Parish, 1½ miles north of Bungay.

3. Published in 1887.

4. 2 Samuel 18 : 33.

5. Kipling's only son, John, was reported missing, believed killed, in 1916, and was never heard of again. [LRH's note.]

6. Quoted from the Litany or General Supplication to be used after the Third Collect at Morning or Evening Prayer; or before the Holy Communion; or separately, in the Protestant Episcopal Church (US) *Book of Common Prayer*.

7. Originally *She*, published in 1887; the new printing of the book (1973) bears the subtitle, *The Life and Love Story of She-who-must-be-obeyed*.

8. Published in 1924.

9. Published in 1926.

10. Published in 1927.

11. Published in 1930.

The Encaenia of 1907[1]

HOWARD G. BAETZHOLD

On the morning of 26 June 1907, under an archway near the Sheldonian Theatre, two men in academic robes puffed on their

* *Oxford Magazine*, LXXV (28 Feb 1957) p. 322.

cigars and reminisced, for as old friends who had not met for some years they had much to discuss. They became so engrossed, in fact, that they had to be summoned for the ceremony.

Lord Curzon of Kedleston,[2] the newly appointed Chancellor, pronounced the citation for each:

Samuelem Langhorne Clemens: *Vir jucundissime, lepidissime, facetissime, qui totius orbis terrarum latera nativa tua hilaritate concutis, ego auctoritate mea et totius Universitatis admitto te ad gradum Doctoris in Litteris honoris causa.*

Rudyardum Kipling: *Vates imperatorie, auctor movendarum lacrimarum ac risuum potentissime, ego etc.*[3]

After each of these awards the applause was tumultuous, despite the fact that Mark Twain and Kipling came last but one in a list of thirty-five honorands. As *The Times* reported 'It was now well past 1 o'clock' (the Convocation had begun shortly after 11 a.m.) 'and if Mr Kipling and Mr Clemens had not been reserved until near the end, there would have been long before a considerable exodus of those who could find an exit.' Kipling himself, only a few months before his death in 1936, recalled that 'When Mark Twain advanced to receive his hood, even those dignified old Oxford dons stood up and yelled.'

Besides the high honour bestowed by Oxford, the Encaenia of 1907 saw the culmination of the long friendship of Kipling and Twain, for they did not meet again before the latter's death in 1910. That friendship had begun in 1889, when the twenty-three-year-old Kipling visited Mark Twain, then fifty-three, in Elmira, New York. Virtually unknown outside of India, Kipling was journeying to England via the United States and felt that he must meet and interview for his newspaper in Allahabad the author whom he 'had learned to love and admire 14,000 miles away' and whom he later considered 'the master of us all'. The vivid report of that interview is included in Kipling's *From Sea to Sea* (1899), and Twain's memories of the event may be found in the volume of his autobiography entitled *Mark Twain in Eruption* (1940). The pair met on numerous occasions thereafter, chiefly during Kipling's American sojourn, 1892–6.

That their mutual esteem was great is undeniable. Many of Twain's letters and also his *Following the Equator*[4] contain allusions to

Kipling and to his work and his strong approval of British rule in India was an unmistakable debt to Kipling's views. Among favourite prose pieces were *Kim* and *The Jungle Book* and, especially in his later years, Twain often entertained his friends with readings from Kipling's poetry. For his part, Kipling, in both his fiction and non-fiction, made reference to Twain's books, notably *Tom Sawyer*, *Huckleberry Finn* and *Life on the Mississippi*. Seven of his short stories show similarities to Twain's writing in style and idea, and *Kim* seems to owe much to *Huckleberry Finn*.

Kipling was always to Mark Twain 'the militant spokesman of the Anglo-Saxon races', whose words stirred him 'more than . . . any other living man's'. At a dinner in the Great Hall of Christ Church, several days after the Encaenia, he referred to Kipling as 'a Prince of the Republic of Letters whose literary fame enveloped the world like an atmosphere'.

Kipling was equally laudatory. In 1903 a letter to Frank Doubleday, his American publisher, exclaimed, 'I love to think of the great and God-like Clemens. He is the biggest man you have on your side of the water.' And in 1935, as chairman of the Mark Twain Centennial Committee in England, he wrote to President Nicholas Murray Butler,[5] of Columbia University, the Committee chairman in America, 'To my mind he was the largest man of his time, both in the direct outcome of his work and, more important still, as an indirect force in an age of iron Philistinism. Later generations do not know their debt'.

The esteem in which Mark Twain is held by literary critics and scholars has never been greater than at present. And although Kipling has been somewhat neglected of late, there have been signs in recent years of an increased scholarly interest in his work.

The University honoured them then: let us honour them now by marking the fiftieth anniversary both of their award and of their last meeting.

NOTES

Professor Baetzhold (b. 1923) is a member of the English Department at Butler University, Indianapolis, Indiana, and a specialist in nineteenth-century Anglo-American literary relations, late nineteenth-century American literature, and American humour. He is working on the Iowa–California Edition of the writings of Mark Twain.

1. An encaenia is a dedication festival at Oxford, or a commemoration.
2. George Nathaniel Curzon, Curzon of Kedleston 1st Marquess (1859–1925),

spent much of his brilliant career on Indian affairs, first as Under-secretary of State for India (1891–2), then as Viceroy of India (1898–1905), and as administrator and reformer on a grand scale. He set up the North-west Frontier Provinces. Partitioning Bengal (1905) angered the Hindus. He headed the House of Lords from 1916 to 1924.

3. 'Samuel Langhorne Clemens: pleasant, charming, and witty, you who make the sides of the whole earth shake with laughter at your native merriment, by my authority and by that of the whole University, I admit you to the degree of honorary doctor of letters.'

'Rudyard Kipling: imperial bard, author most potent at moving tears and laughter, by my . . . .'

4. Published in 1909.

5. American educator (1862–1947); Butler became President of Columbia University in 1902. He was an unsuccessful candidate for the vice-presidency on the Republican ticket in 1912. President of the Carnegie Endowment for International Peace, 1925–45. Co-winner (in 1931) of the Nobel Peace Prize.

'Kipling Is Not the Meekest of Men'*

JEROME K. JEROME

'*The Idler*. Edited by Jerome K. Jerome and Robert Barr.¹ An illustrated monthly magazine, price sixpence', was Barr's idea. But the title was mine. Barr had made the English edition of the *Detroit Free Press* quite a good property; and was keen to start something of his own. He wanted a popular name and, at first, was undecided between Kipling and myself. He chose me – as, speaking somewhat bitterly, he later on confessed to me – thinking I should be the easier to 'manage'. He had not liked the look of Kipling's jaw. Kipling had been about two years in London, and had just married his secretary, a beautiful girl with a haunting melancholy in her eyes that still lingers.

By writers he was recognised as a new force, though his aggressive personality naturally made enemies. The critics and the public were

* *My Life and Times* (New York and London: Harper, 1926) pp. 166–7, 232–3.

more squeamish then. He was accused of coarseness and irreverence. The reason, it is said, that he was never knighted was that Queen Victoria would not forgive him for having called her 'The Widdy o' Windsor'. He has not missed much. Lord Charles Beresford[2] used to tell the story – and those who knew him could easily believe it – that King Edward on one occasion said to him 'You remember L—, that fellow at Homburg. Well, I've just made him a knight.'

'Dirty little bounder', said Beresford; 'serve him damn well right.' . . .

The amateur photographer is the curse of Switzerland. One would not mind if they took one at one's best. There was a charming photograph in *The Sphere* one winter of my daughter and myself, waltzing on the ice at Grindelwald.[3] It made a pretty picture. But, as a rule, beauty does not appeal to the snap-shotter. I noticed, in my early skiing days, that whenever I did anything graceful the Kodak crowd was always looking the other way. When I was lying on my back with my feet in the air, the first thing I always saw when I recovered my senses, was a complete circle of Kodaks pointing straight at me. Poor Rudyard Kipling never got a chance of learning. I was at Engelberg[4] with him one winter. He was in the elementary stage as regards both skating and skiing; and wherever he went the Kodak fiends followed him in their hundreds. He must have felt like a comet trying to lose its own tail.

I took him one morning to a skiing ground I had discovered some mile or more away: an ideal spot for the beginner. We started early and thought we had escaped them. But some fool had seen us, and had given the hulloa; and before we had got on our skis, half Engelberg was pouring down the road.

Kipling is not the meekest of men and I marvelled at his patience.

'They might give me a start', he sighed; 'I would like to have had them on, just once.'

Engelberg is too low to be a good sports centre. We had some muggy weather, and to kill time I got up some private theatricals. Kipling's boy and girl were there. They were jolly children. Young Kipling was a suffragette and little Miss Kipling played a costermonger's donah. Kipling himself combined the parts of scene-shifter and call boy. It was the first time I had met Mrs Kipling since her marriage. She was still a beautiful woman, but her hair was white. There had always been sadness in her eyes, even when a girl. The Hornungs were there also, with their only child, Oscar. Mrs Hornung, *née* Connie Doyle,[5] was as cheery and vigorous as ever, but a shade stouter. Both boys were killed in the war.

It was election time in England, and the hotel crowd used to encourage Kipling and myself to political argument in the great hall. I suppose I was the only man in the hotel who was not a die-hard conversative. Kipling himself was always courteous, but not all the peppery old colonels from Cheltenham and fierce old ladies from Bath were. Notwithstanding, on wet afternoons, when one couldn't go out, it wasn't bad sport.

NOTES

English novelist, dramatist, and humorist (1859–1927), Jerome will be re-membered for a long time as the author of *Three Men in a Boat* (1889) and *The Passing of the Third Floor Back* (1908).

1. Born in Glasgow in 1850, Barr taught in schools in Canada until 1876. He wrote all kinds of essays and fiction; was a prolific novelist; and achieved a considerable reputation as an editor.

2. Charles William de la Poer, 1st Baron Beresford (1846–1919), participated in the bombardment of Alexandria (1882) and the Nile Expedition (1884–5), as well as various battles in the Sudan. He achieved distinction as both an admiral and as a parliamentarian.

3. Village in central Switzerland, south-eastern part of the canton of Bern, with a famous view of the mountains of the Bernese Oberland.

4. Health resort in central Switzerland, in the half-canton of Obwalden; a popular sports centre.

5. Constance Doyle, daughter of Charles Altamont Doyle, and granddaughter of John Doyle; wife of Ernest William Hornung, novelist and journalist.

Rudyard Kipling as I Knew Him*

G. A. BALLARD

When I accepted an invitation to join the Kipling Society I was informed that personal reminiscences of him were much in request among its members, and I am very pleased therefore to meet the desire of the Editor to contribute some account of my own experiences in that respect for its journal.

My first acquaintance with Rudyard Kipling was only brief and superficial. It was in 1898 when he was the private guest of the captain of a cruiser in the same squadron as a ship in which I was myself a commander. His host was merely taking him around on a series of visits to each vessel.

But during the early part of the first World War I saw a good deal of him at close quarters. He was writing on various aspects of the war for one of the leading London daily papers under official sanction, and received special facilities from the Admiralty. I was Admiral in command of the East Coast patrol forces at that time and was ordered to receive him as my official guest for a specified period during which he was to be allowed to get an idea of our work without disclosing confidential matter. He arrived on board my flagship accordingly and for more than a week occupied the spare cabin and sat at my table with my personal staff and self. And of course he made the acquaintance of the other officers on board. At first a slight reserve existed on both sides. For our part, we were somewhat impressed by finding such a celebrity among us; and he, to begin with, rather felt the novelty of his surroundings I think, as he was diffident in manner, and in fact almost deferential towards me. But all that soon wore off, and we were all on a very sociable and easy footing before he departed. In leaving he spoke to me in

* *Kipling Journal*, XIII (Oct 1946) 3–5.

most appreciative terms about his stay on board with such obvious
sincerity that I am convinced he enjoyed it. I know that I did. We
had a laugh together over his problem of producing articles to
interest the public when all the really interesting points in the work
of the patrols were strictly secret. However he possessed in a
remarkable degree the gift of making the most of any subject he
chose to write about, and I found that reading it was almost more
absorbing than the subject itself in this case, though the subject was
not without its excitements. He would have liked to mix with the
men forward, and I told him he might if he wished, but that I
doubted if they would talk with complete freedom to anybody they
knew to be a semi-official guest in the Admiral's quarters. He quite
saw that point and decided to remain aft.

When he left I lost touch with him till a fairly long time after the
war. I had retired from the Navy and I believe he was no longer
connected directly with journalism. But we were both members of
the Society for Nautical Research, in whose activities he took a close
interest, and through which he started a correspondence with me,
lasting on and off till near his end. He wrote to me that he was
attracted by the little he had heard about life in the Navy in
Victorian days but never had the chance to be sufficiently
acquainted with it to use it properly in literature. He put a whole
series of questions to me on the subject, as having lived in it. I was
only too pleased to respond, especially as in this renewal of
intercourse the approach had come from his side when I had
presumed that he had probably forgotten all about me. Apparently
he was considering the idea of some nautical tales, and being always
anxious to avoid 'howlers', felt the truth of Southey's observation
that a landsman writing on nautical affairs 'had to tread as carefully
as a cat in a china pantry'. Thus he would scarcely have committed
Stevenson's absurdity in *Treasure Island* where the secret position of
the buried loot is indicated by a precision in longitude equivalent to
measuring the width of the Atlantic in feet, at a period in history
when no means existed of obtaining it with more accuracy than the
nearest thirty miles. It was not that Kipling never tripped up at all,
but his mistakes were few and confined to his earlier works when he
confessed to less care. He asked me to point them out and thanked
his stars that his reviewers had never served at sea.

But he did acquire a very good knowledge in one way or another of
technical sea language, and would spend hours for instance on a
ship's bridge or in the engine-room. Complex and powerful

machinery seemed to fascinate him, and he always insisted on its genuine but commonly unrecognised romance. It was this side of his genius that produced 'McAndrew's Hymn', in which Kipling's free use of highly technical language is faultless throughout. Again in his short story 'The Ship that Found Herself'[1] he went all out in nautical terms and never slipped up once either in the actual words or their correct application. It was the same in his treatment of the major aspects of seafaring existence, as in 'The Merchantman'.[2] His line 'We dipped our gunnels under to the dread Agulhas roll' is a fine instance of an understanding that brought a grim chuckle of appreciation from many ancient mariners as a reminder of a night passed under close-reefed sails in a roaring south-wester on the Agulhas Bank, one of the stormiest stretches of water in the whole world. I have been through that experience and can testify to the vivid insight of the allusion. Possibly it does not mean so much to modern seamen, as all steamer tracks lie inshore of the Bank. Moreover a steamer can meet a heavy sea bows on, whereas a vessel lying-to under sail must take its buffets in her ribs, and 'dips her gunnels under' accordingly. Unfortunately on some occasions they dipped too far to come up again. I dwell on this as a professional seaman of the old school to emphasise Kipling's remarkable realisation of the conditions of our existence and occupation sixty years ago at sea.

And if ships and their gear attracted his attention, it was attracted still more by the sort of men to be found on board, if the questions he put to me were any indication. He seemed particularly curious to know what sort of contact existed between midshipmen of school-boy age (as they were in Victorian times) and the much older petty officers and men placed under their authority in many situations, especially in a boat away from the ship when all responsibility for handling the boat and the boat's crew lay with the midshipman in charge. I told him that the men soon sized up the qualities of these officers in command, and that speaking from personal experience it was uncommonly good training for the midshipman in the ways of both boats and blue-jackets, in which they learnt lessons they were never likely to forget. This seemed to tickle RK.

No doubt it is unnecessary to inform members of the Kipling Society that he was a man of very varied tastes and interests. But as I have been invited to tell what I knew of him, I may perhaps just mention his fondness for dogs. He was greatly taken by a yarn of mine about the rescue of a spaniel belonging to me when I commanded the cruiser *Hampshire*, which, although not gun-shy in the field, did nevertheless jump overboard at sea on the first occasion of being terrified by the noise and shaking of heavy-gun-practice in the ship, and always had to be locked below when that took place afterwards.

Kipling sometimes liked to indulge in a fanciful manner of expressing himself. As an instance, he acquired a copy of the International Flag Signal Book, which before the invention of wireless telegraphy was freely used by the ships of all countries for communicating with each other at sea or with Lloyds signal stations, in the days when vessels were often on voyages lasting unbroken for months. Meetings in mid-ocean between two such, nearly always meant an interchange of the signal 'Do you report all well?" The book has a coloured plate showing all the flags with the letter of the alphabet or the numeral figure each represents. One day a letter came to me, on the envelope of which I recognised his handwriting, but on opening was mystified to find a first sheet entirely covered by a display of hand-painted flags, which I eventually discovered could be read as that same signal. He repeated that little joke two or three times afterwards, on each occasion with a different signal.

But the last letter I had from him was very brief and not jocular. He simply asked me to accept as a gift an autographed copy of his latest published work; and I have sometimes rather wondered whether he felt that even if his end was not imminent, it might not be far off.

I never was in touch with Kipling's private life nor he with mine. Our contact was entirely associated with matters of interest outside domestic circles, though in that form it extended, with only occasional lapses, over twenty years. To me he seemed to combine strong views, honestly formed, with a modest and unaffected personality and a fine sense of humour. Of course he could not help being aware of the favourable publicity of his name in many countries; but I do not think that held much place in his thoughts, and it never seemed to affect his outlook. I believe he was about the last man in the world to be influenced by public popularity, which is perhaps just one of the reasons it came to him.

NOTES

Admiral George Alexander Ballard, CB (1862–1948), entered the Royal Navy in 1875. He was in the Battle of Tamai, near Suakim (1884); Burma (1885–6); and the

Boxer Rising in China (1900). He served, among several other important assignments, as Director of Operations Division, Admiralty War Staff. He wrote studies of naval policy in Japan, America's role in the Atlantic, and naval forces in the Indian Ocean.

1. First published in the *Bombay Gazette* (?), 1895, and *The Idler*, Dec 1895; collected in *The Day's Work* (1898).

2. First printed in the *Pall Mall Budget*, 15 May 1894; collected in *The Seven Seas* (1896).

Mr Kipling*

LUCY HILTON

'The Elms', home of Mr and Mrs Rudyard Kipling and their three children, John, Josephine and Elsie. Mr Kipling was at his best when with his children and their playmates; he had a large sand-garden made for their delight which they played in when not able to get to the beach. One of their little friends, Molly Stanford, told me Mrs Kipling grew gourds and cut the initials of each child upon a different gourd, and each day they would watch to see whose initials had grown largest. They were so happy and safe in that high walled garden, and were taken each day to visit Aunt Georgiana who was Lady Burne-Jones and lived just across the Pump Green. Mr Kipling had a charming lady named Miss Anderson who was his secretary and she lived in rooms opposite the Black Horse just above the surgery of Dr Ridsdale. I used to run errands for her and tidy up her room and make her fire. One day she was expecting Mr Kipling to call with his work for typing. She asked me to make the fire. I tried very hard to get it to burn before he came as I did not want to be in the room at the time, he rather scared me with his thick spectacles and black eyebrows and very quick movement. Presently I heard that quick step coming upstairs and enter the sitting-room. After talking to Miss Anderson, he looked down at me and said sharply, 'What are you doing child?' and I answered, 'Lighting the fire, sir.' He said, 'Not making a very good job of it are you? Give me some paper', which I did. He rolled some little paper balls and said, 'Put them underneath the stick', which I did, and soon the fire

* *Kipling Journal*, xxxvi (Mar 1969) 14–17.

burned and I scuttled out of the room. I remember seeing stacks of
'The Absent-minded Beggar' upon Miss Anderson's desk and of
course we children could have as many as we liked for the asking,
but did not realise how famous was the man who had written that
poem and many others whilst living in Rottingdean. Mr Kipling
visited his Aunt, Lady Burne-Jones, many times before he came to
live here and when he did settle down we were told he wrote books
and poetry. In a small village the interest grows quickly. He was
always in a hurry and if he wanted a cab to take him to Brighton
Station five miles away, he always kept the driver waiting, and the
driver had to break 'the speed limit' to catch the train. Soon he
began to take an interest in the village and its people. He was easily
aroused to anger but we were willing to make friends as time went
on. One day he was taking Mrs Kipling out in his car. Yes, he had a
car, an American buckboard with a bell on it, not a horn, also a
chauffeur, who was driving at the time. On reaching Pax or
Downlands[1] as it was called at the time, the car stopped and
Lawrence couldn't do a thing about it. Mr Kipling got out of the car
and began pacing the pavement, then he looked up at Mrs Kipling
and said 'Carrie, my dear, American women are the best in the
world. But American cars, damn 'em!' His next car was a
Lanchester. Many people came into the village to catch a glimpse of
him as his fame was steadily growing. It is said he disliked the public
and didn't want to see them.

I was walking by the pond one morning when Mr Kipling came
along; coming towards him were some visitors who asked him to
direct them to the Elms. He pointed it out to them and smilingly
passed on. I don't believe they recognised the great man. On the
high wall which surrounds the Elms garden ivy grew, and visitors
used to take pieces away with them as mementos of Kipling's home.
Inside the south and west walls tall trees grew and overhung the
road outside. The village horse buses toured around the streets to
pick up passengers before proceeding to Brighton; one of the
conductors was Charles Tuppen, the champion straight-horn
blower of the world. He was dressed in a long hunting-coat and top-
hat. It was quite a sight to see the bus well kept and the fine horses
being driven by men who had done this job for years, and the horn
being blown so perfectly. Mostly the tunes were connected with
horses and hunting. There was a roadway by the Elms garden at this
time so that the bus passed the wall in front of the house. There were
no tops to the buses so the tall trees of the Elms met the top

passengers and frequently knocked off their hats. Mr Thomas who owned the buses received complaints about these trees, arranged with the driver and conductor to stop the bus and break off the offending branches. Unfortunately at the precise moment of action, Mr Kipling was at an upstairs window watching the proceedings. He ran out, but the bus was on its way. Mr Kipling wrote a stern letter to Mr Thomas, blaming him for the damage to his trees. His gardener's boy duly delivered the letter to the Royal Oak and it was handed to Mr Thomas. On reading the letter he laughed loudly and some customers who were in the lounge at the time said, 'Don't keep it to yourself, read it out and let us join in the fun!' So Mr Thomas read the letter to them; two strangers asked if he would sell the letter to them as a memento and it was settled that the agreed price should be 30 shillings and was cheerfully paid. An attempted repeat failed after more branches from the trees had been removed because Mr Kipling met Mr Thomas in the street and proceeded to voice his displeasure, whereupon Mr Thomas said, 'Look here, sir, I would much rather you sent me some more letters. I can sell them for 30 shillings each.' So the incident ended with a good laugh all round.

Then followed the formation of the Rifle Club. Mr Kipling, Mr Stanford of St Aubyn's School and Mr Mason of Rottingdean School, arranged a meeting for the men of the village. Many joined and rifles were purchased. Mr Kipling leased the field where the Convent of St Martha stands and soon a room was built that could be used as an indoor shooting-range and later the girls of the village used it for physical exercises and gymnastics. For some time past rumours of war were heard from one of the colonies, South Africa. There was trouble in the great mining areas. People seemed to know very little about what was going on in a place so far away but we were advised to be prepared. Our riflemen got busy getting to understand their weapons: the Lee Metford and Lee Enfield and Morris tubes for the indoor shooting. Living in the village were Sergeant Johnson and Sergeant Rose, both on the retired list. Johnson was a fairly young man who retired from service because of an injured leg which caused him to walk with a limp. He was a splendid drill sergeant and soon had a fine squad of men ready for any emergencies. Sergeant Rose and the coastguards also helped in this good work of drilling and shooting. In the team were many crack shots, G. Mason, F. Wheeler, A. E. Coe, H. Sladescone, J. Cook and others. Club matches were arranged between the rifle clubs of other districts, so for the young men of the village much excitement had come their way. The outdoor shooting-range began at the top of East Hill from the Whiteway Road and the firing-points began in stages down the hill. The top was 1000 yards from the target, then followed 800, 600, 500, 300 and 200 yards. A hut was specially built in the valley because of the hollow in the ground. Now the target butts were dug out on the opposite side of the hill where a pulley arrangement was installed which caused one target to go up whilst the other to go down, and men were on duty with these targets to signal where the bullet went by placing discs on the spots, and also during firing-practice a large red flag was displayed to warn approaching travellers. Now Mr Kipling was very keen about the shooting and was seldom absent. He took his turn with the rest. One Friday afternoon, the men were shooting from the 600-yard firing-point. Two men were waiting their turn, lying on the ground with rifles ready. A shout went up. There were people walking into the firing-line. Mr Kipling was angry as the red flag was up to warn them. He shouted at them through the megaphone but they still walked forward. Mr Kipling brought his binoculars into play. After surveying the scene he said, 'It's all right, they don't live in Rottingdean, they are wearing cuffs.' Once Mr Kipling and F. Wheeler were ready to fire from the same point and he noticed F. Wheeler rubbing his fingers, as much flexibility is needed for shooting. Mr Kipling wanted to know the reason for the finger-rubbing and F. Wheeler told him he had been exercising horses for his father, who trained them for racing, and one of the horses was a rough pulling animal and had made his fingers stiff and sore. Nothing more was said about the incident, but Mr Kipling had not forgotten, and some time after he wrote about the various members of the Rifle Club and any peculiarities they possessed. Wheeler's lines ran as follows:

> The trainer's son on a pulling horse
> It is bad for the trigger finger.

It was published in the *Spectator*. As well as a very efficient rifle club Mr Kipling procured a machine-gun called 'Maxim Nordenfeldt' which was pulled with ropes to the cliff-edge and fired into the sea. We really felt fully armed with this added protection. By this time the South African War was being fought and we were naturally very thrilled at the exploits of our troops. Mr Kipling was writing poetry, urging young men to join up. He was doing all he could to raise funds for war charities. At a concert in the village school Mr Kipling recited one of his poems called 'The Absent-minded Beggar'. The audience were very enthusiastic and money was showered on the platform. Another of Mr Kipling's poems was intended to stimulate recruiting. He referred to cricketers and footballers as muddied oafs and flannelled fools.[2] It wasn't very well liked in some quarters. The war was drawing to a close by this time. The news reached us that Mafeking was relieved. Some of our troops had been beleaguered in this place for some time, surrounded by the enemy. When the news came to us, it was late in the evening and the rejoicing was tremendous – shouting and singing in the street, bell-ringing and all the usual celebrations took place. At last the end of the war was declared and our Rifle Club members, although ready and willing, were not required. But interest in the war was aroused again when a strange thing happened, and very soon everyone knew that on the outside of North End House appeared a broad white banner across one part of the house. On it was printed in large black letters this message: 'We have killed and also taken possession.' Towards evening the village grape-vine having done its work, everyone came to the roadway and the village-green to see this announcement and to find out the meaning. Soon there were grumbles and growls and shouts of 'Burn it down.' When Mr Ridsdale came from the Dene to enquire into the disturbance, he was talking to the men and explaining the message when Mr Kipling came striding across the Green, and called for members of the Rifle Club who were present to help keep order. Soon the anger died down when the two gentlemen went into the house and soon the offending poster was removed. Lady Burne-Jones hated war and all the misery it entailed, and the poster was in protest against it. The villagers drifted away home and the next day all was quiet and no one worried about the banner . . . . In 1902 Mr Kipling left the village, after living in Rottingdean for five years. It seems a short stay but he stirred up the people here, especially the men. We were interested in all he did and those who knew him will never forget the impact he made. He bought a lovely house at Burwash in Sussex which is opened to the public during part of the year.

To his memory was built the Church of the Recessional at Forest Lawn Memorial Park, Glendale, California. To the life and works of the great soldier poet Rudyard Kipling. This church is a perfect reproduction of the parish church of St Margaret's in Rottingdean where Mr Kipling was inspired to write his famous poem 'Recessional'.

NOTES

This selection comes from an unpublished manuscript entitled 'Memories of Old Rottingdean'.

1. Seat in East Sussex, ½ mile north-north-west of Uckfield.

2. A reference to 'The Islanders', first published in the *Weekly Times*, 3 Jan 1902, and collected in *The Five Nations* (1903).

Dramatising 'The Story of the Gadsbys'*

COSMO HAMILTON

My association with Kipling began when I was young and perhaps because of this, and with the remembrance of his own precocity, he was very kind to me. I had written a play or two which had found their way to the stage, and one or two young novels which had had their little day. I could no more remember their titles now than fly over the moon. I loved and admired Kipling, had sung those of the Barrack-Room Ballads to which lilting tunes had been set while on the march with the cadet corps with which I trained for years – usefully as it happened according to the ways of Fate – and became obsessed with a desire to dramatise 'The Story of the Gadsbys',[1] though I dared not mention it. For months I nursed this pain, this secret and growing urge, until an optimistic morning sent my courage up. Before it could grow cold and leave me in the shade I dashed to pen and ink, wrote a letter to Kipling, begged him to permit me to have a shot at it and dropped it in the box. I expected to hear nothing, though I prayed that I might. I could see my letter diverted from the master by a scoffing secretary. For two whole days I suffered from an attack of bated breath. Then came a blue card in a neat blue envelope and on the card in the small neat writing of the man whose work I loved the following thrilling words: 'I've had several shots at it but my efforts have been awful and I've chucked 'em all

* *People Worth Talking About* (New York: Robert M. McBride, 1933) pp. 25–8.

away. If you think you can do the trick, go ahead, my lad. I'm off to South Africa at the end of this month and if you can finish it two days before I sail send it to me here. Good luck. – RK.'

By working all day and far into the night, by having my meals brought to my desk while I wrote, cut and rewrote in a spell of concentration in what was a labour of love, by cutting myself off from the routine of my house, ignoring letters and telephone-calls and living like a monk, I did finish it. But in the process of dramatisation it was necessary, as it always is, to take liberties with the story, to introduce new people, to elaborate the main theme and to bring out one of the characters in bas-relief to the rest. I made Gadsby and not his little bride the leading part in the play, dear old heavy-footed Gadsby who maintained his bachelor point of view even after the wedding-bells had turned his spine to ice. And in order to bring down the second-act curtain on a strong dramatic scene I invented a situation which the story hadn't contained.

It was with the utmost trepidation, therefore, that I sent off the play and waited for Kipling's verdict with ice in my own spine. For one strange day I played golf, slicing and pulling every drive and muffing all my putts. Then came the neat blue envelope and another neat blue card and in the small neat writing of the wizard of the East words that turned my heart. 'Your shot has hit the bull,' he wrote, 'and you have done the trick. Go ahead and place the play and good luck again. – RK.' The play was sent by Kipling's agent to Harrison and Maude, the famous Cyril Maude[2] who had revived the glory of the Haymarket Theatre with a long series of hits. It was accepted with emotion and a contract was signed at once, so that after his arrival in South Africa to stay with Cecil Rhodes, 50 per cent of the preliminary payment dropped out of his agent's envelope on Kipling's breakfast plate. My game of golf was sound again and I sank most of my putts.

It is difficult to understand why Kipling has ignored the stage, or why he hasn't ever made a magnificent pageant of *Kim*. There isn't the slightest doubt that, if he chose to do so, he could write fine plays and it is on the cards that one wet day he may turn his mind to it. Another fame will be his.

The last time I saw RK was in London at Brown's Hotel. I had called there to see some Boston friends of mine. It is the most old-fashioned of all the London hotels and is for that reason the most comfortable and agreeable of them all – not unlike a country house in the middle of Mayfair, with a butler who is probably the model of

P. G. Wodehouse's Jeeves. One is never a mere number there but is known by one's name. It is the only place in London in which Kipling ever stays, though he rarely leaves the solitude of his charming country house. The important moment had come, it appeared, when it was necessary for him to choose and buy a new typewriting machine. He had obviously sent out chits and so men had arrived with samples which they had placed in the sitting-room. On every available table these glistening black things stood, each with its eager representative from the office of its birth. The room was filled with people who were killing time till lunch. Imagine their excitement when, like a strong east wind, Kipling appeared suddenly and sat in unself-conscious concentration before, in quick succession, each of these machines. Unaware of the interest and amusement which this technical process caused he played first one and then another with a firm and expert touch. Having come to a decision he went with twitching eyebrows and a rap of busy heels into the dining room. What a mob there was for those sheets of paper which he had left in those glistening things! But he was not so unself-conscious as he had appeared to be, because on all those slips he had typed merely a sort of cryptogram. He was not dispensing gems!

NOTES

Born Cosmo Gibbs, Hamilton (1898–1940) assumed his mother's name. He worked with Lord Roberts on the NSL; edited *The World*; and wrote a very large number of plays, novels and memoirs.

1. No. 2 of the Indian Railway Library, consisting of one poem and eight chapters or stories. First published in 1888.

2. English actor–manager (1862–1951); joint manager of the Haymarket Theatre, London (1896–1905). Manager of the Playhouse until 1915. Appeared on stage in both England and the United States, and after 1913, in motion-pictures.